HOSPITALITY SALES: SELLING SMARTER

HOSPITALITY SALES: SELLING SMARTER

by

Judy A. Siguaw
Cornell University
School of Hotel Administration

and

David C. Bojanic
University of Massachusetts at Amherst
Department of Hospitality and Tourism Management

THOMSON

DELMAR LEARNING

Australia Canada Mexico Singapore Spain United Kingdom United States

Hospitality Sales: Selling Smarter
By Judy A. Siguaw and David C. Bojanic

Vice President, Career Education Strategic Business Unit:
Dawn Gerrain

Director of Editorial:
Sherry Gomoll

Senior Acquisitions Editor:
Joan M. Gill

Editorial Assistant:
Lisa Flatley

Director of Production:
Wendy A. Troeger

Production Manager:
Carolyn Miller

Production Editor:
Matthew J. Williams

Project Editor:
Maureen M.E. Grealish

Channel Manager:
Wendy E. Mapstone

Cover Image:
Image Ideas

Library of Congress Cataloging-in-Publication Data

ISBN 1-4018-3478-7

NOTICE TO THE READER

CONTENTS

v

PREFACE

ales skills are the most critical abilities any professional can possess. To be successful, professional people must know how to sell their abilities to supervisors, to influence subordinates to follow their plans of action, and to convince investors and customers regarding their products and services. Indeed, as business people we constantly are placed in selling situations in both our professional and personal lives. Unfortunately, we are not always as effective as we would like to be. *Hospitality Sales: Selling Smarter* is designed to improve our sales effectiveness.

This book is a culmination of decades of working, teaching, and researching in the field of sales. The material presented herein has been tested over the years, refined, and proven to effectively train professionals and college students in sales. Furthermore, the book is intended to serve as a complementary resource for individuals seeking to earn accreditation in hospitality sales and marketing through the Hospital Sales and Marketing Association International (HSMAI). Consequently, we have taken these seminar and classroom materials and combined them into a manuscript that presents a systematic, practical approach to hospitality sales, with an emphasis on honing actual consultative sales skills. By using these skills, readers can move from pushing their products and services to addressing customer needs, adapting to customer communication styles, and personalizing the sales presentation based on the benefits of greatest interest to each customer.

This book offers a number of benefits. Written in a workbook style to reinforce ideas, the book effectively blends sales concepts and theories with practical exercises to assist the reader in applying the lessons learned and enhancing understanding. Ten chapters are devoted to the sales process to ensure that the reader improves selling skills, thus increases productivity, performance, and income. Further, because of the emphasis on learning critical sales skills, the reader can immediately utilize these skills in his or her current job, as well as future positions. Finally, the book is written in an easy-to-read style for time-pressed sales professionals and is designed for those who work specifically within the hospitality industry, so readers can readily relate to the material.

This book is a practical, hands-on tool for sales professionals, sales novices, and students. It covers the entire sales process from prospecting to follow-up after the sale, and also includes chapters on time management, contracts, meeting services, negotiation, and revenue management. Thus, this book can be used to train new salespeople and to serve as a refresher course for more experienced hospitality sales professionals. This digest would work equally well for individuals who are seeking to improve their sales skills on their own, or for groups of salespeople who are working with a "trainer." Certainly, this book can be a valuable resource for any independent or smaller property where corporate sales training is absent or minimal. Similarly, it serves as a wonderful resource and provides additional reinforcement in those situations where formal sales training is available.

ACKNOWLEDGMENTS

Special thanks to Kevin, Stephanie, Trish and Christine who make me happy and remind me of what is important in life.

I would like to thank my son, Matthew, and the rest of my family for their dedication and support.

Delmar Learning and the authors would also like to thank the following reviewers for their valuable input:

Michael G. Brizek, FMP, CHE
University of Maryland Eastern Shore

Edward A. Merritt, Ph.D.
California State University (Cal Poly Pomona)

Joseph M. La Lopa
Purdue University

Dr. Evangelos Christou
Technological Educational Institute of Thessaloniki , Greece

Roger Gerard
Shasta College

1

Overview of
Hospitality Sales

Importance of Selling

The sales function is the cornerstone of the hospitality industry. Those employed in hospitality sales are directly responsible for the revenues of their respective organizations. Consequently, hospitality firms allocate more funds to personal selling than to any other promotional tool.

Organizations are willing to make large investments in personal selling because, not only does it result in income for the firm, but sales efforts also increase customer satisfaction. Personal selling is the only promotional form that offers immediate feedback, allowing sales people to adapt continuously so that the needs of each individual customer are addressed. That is, personal selling has the highest level of flexibility of all promotional methods and allows for micro-marketing—marketing to "one."

This introductory chapter first discusses consultative sales, the sales approach advocated. Next, the traits commonly found in good salespeople are identified and the various sales in hospitality are described. Finally, each step of the sales process; which will be elaborated on in this book; is introduced.

Consultative vs. Traditional Selling

In this book, **personal selling** is defined as person-to-person communication with a prospective customer in order to develop a relationship, identify customer needs, match goods/services with those needs, communicate benefits to customers, and gain commitment to purchase goods/services that satisfy customer needs. This definition advocates a consultative selling approach. Consultative selling focuses on satisfying the needs of the customer; thus, consultative salespeople seek to act as problem-solvers. As shown in the comparative table in Figure 1-1, Consultative Selling vs. Traditional Selling, a consultative sales approach concentrates most of its efforts in the early stages of the sales process: preapproach, approach, and need identification. The emphasis is on information gathering and dissemination. Consequently, the consultative salesperson is able to establish a relationship with the prospect, concentrate on the needs of the prospective customer, and readily handle any objections. In doing so, gaining commitment from the prospect is natural and easy. By contrast, traditional sales approaches focus most heavily on the latter stages of the sales process. As a result, little effort is made to understand the needs of the prospective customer; thus, handling objections is difficult and closing the sale is more complex, artificial, and time-consuming. In essence, all customers are treated as if they have the same needs.

Consultative selling is best used in conjunction with strategic sales planning.[1] The integration of consultative and strategic selling has evolved in response to today's hyper-competitive environment, the increase in the complexity of services/goods, and the growing emphasis on relationship marketing. In using this integrated approach, salespeople first utilize customer mapping to understand the critical roles that are involved in the buying decision process.

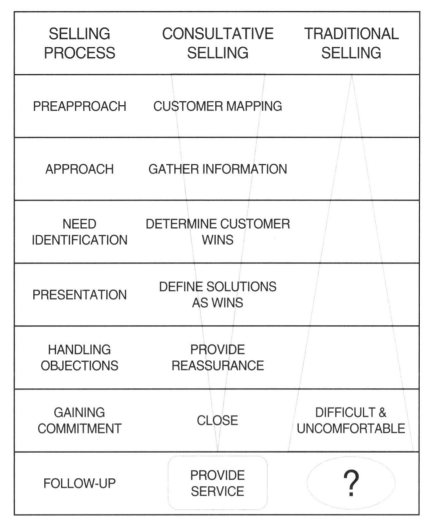

SELLING PROCESS	CONSULTATIVE SELLING	TRADITIONAL SELLING
PREAPPROACH	CUSTOMER MAPPING	
APPROACH	GATHER INFORMATION	
NEED IDENTIFICATION	DETERMINE CUSTOMER WINS	
PRESENTATION	DEFINE SOLUTIONS AS WINS	
HANDLING OBJECTIONS	PROVIDE REASSURANCE	
GAINING COMMITMENT	CLOSE	DIFFICULT & UNCOMFORTABLE
FOLLOW-UP	PROVIDE SERVICE	?

Figure 1-1 Consultative Selling vs. Traditional Selling

The first step is followed by information gathering, the determination of customer needs, the development of solutions as "wins," the provision of reassurances, the close, and finally, the provision of after-sale service. This book emphasizes this blended approach.

As you might suspect, this approach to selling also encourages **relationship selling**, in which the salesperson seeks the development of a trusting partnership with the customer as a means of providing long-term customer understanding and satisfaction. When utilizing relationship selling, customers benefit by having their needs anticipated and met, while the salesperson gains future sales that are yielded from the relationship over time. Because the cost of obtaining a new customer is much greater than the cost of retaining a current customer, the goal of every salesperson should be to develop long-term relationships with customers.

Characteristics of a Good Salesperson

Good salespeople have a number of common traits, as shown in Figure 1-2, Desirable Salesperson Traits. They are self-motivated, organized, enthusiastic, competitive, goal-oriented, empathetic listeners, and most importantly, adaptive and learning-oriented, and customer-oriented. **Adaptive** salespeople have the ability to routinely alter the way they communicate, so they match the communication styles of their customers.[2] In turn, these salespeople are more effective communicators, which aids in developing customer rapport and presenting the right information to each customer. **Learning-oriented** sales people are open to and excited about acquiring new knowledge or skills.[3] **Customer-oriented** means the salesperson seeks to resolve customer problems in a manner that is in the best interest of the customer, rather than seeking to sell a product or service that may not truly meet the needs of the customer.[4] These latter traits have been identified as the differentiating factors between successful and mediocre salespeople.[5]

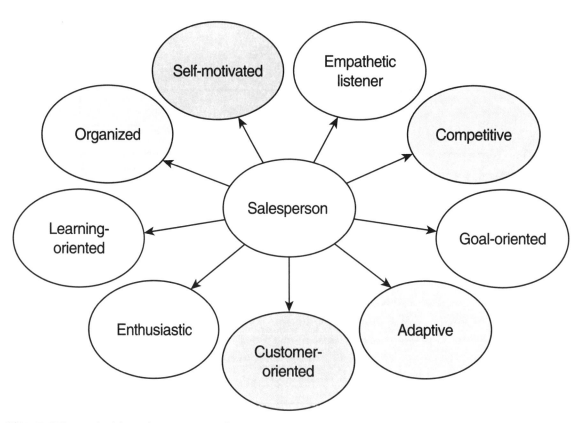

Figure 1-2 Desirable Salesperson Traits

Sales Roles in Hospitality

Hospitality organizations may structure their sales departments in diverse fashions. The structures may be determined by many factors, including the size of the organization, the size of the property, the property segment (budget/economy, mid-scale, upscale, luxury), and the property type (such as, convention hotel, resort, casino). Career opportunities in sales are available in nearly all property segments, sizes, and types. However, an increase in the complexity of hotel operations will likely lead to greater complexity in the sales department, with each line function holding different responsibilities.[6]

Directors of marketing are senior-level managers responsible for governing the sales and marketing efforts of the organization. They formulate long-term goals, direct the sales strategy, determine the marketing and sales budgets, and oversee advertising. In some organizations, the directors of marketing at the property level may have responsibilities equivalent to corporate sales managers at other organizations. If the size of their respective organizations warrant it, the directors of marketing may have several department heads that fall under their direct supervision. These department heads may include director of group sales, director of transient sales, and director of catering.

A **Director of group sales** oversees the group room sales effort of the senior and junior salespeople, and is personally responsible for maintaining and growing key group accounts. A **Director of transient sales** supervises the reservationists and is accountable for meeting revenue management goals. A **Director of catering** is responsible for the operational catering staff, as well as the sales efforts of the catering staff.

Underneath these department heads are the positions that in turn report to them: senior sales managers, sales managers, transient sales managers, catering managers, and reservationists. **Senior sales managers** (or national account managers) are responsible for calling on key accounts and also serve as mentors to inexperienced sales managers. In some cases, senior sales managers may head their entire sales department. **Sales managers** are the salespeople responsible for group business within assigned market segments. They are often responsible for small- to medium-sized accounts. **Transient sales managers** are the individuals responsible for working with organizations and associations within the local area in order to generate additional transient business. In some cases the transient sales manager will offer special rates to local corporations that can guarantee a certain number of room nights within a specified time frame. **Catering managers** sell to groups whose main function is centered around a catered meal. These local groups frequently do not book any rooms or may book only a small number of rooms. **Reservationists** also function as part of the sales structure of the hospitality firm, but may not be housed within the same department. In recent years, the importance of reservationists has been realized, as they interact with approximately 80 percent of a company's customers.[7] Consequently, reservationists are now receiving better sales training and are being provided with resources and incentives to encourage up-selling and cross-selling. Depending on the size and structure of the hospitality firm, other sales positions beyond the ones noted may be a part of the firm's organizational chart.

While the sales forces of most hospitality firms are still based on-site at the hotel property, some firms are recognizing the importance of being "customer-centric." Some organizations are placing salespeople in locations where their major customers originate rather than where the hospitality firms are located. These salespeople are based from their homes and they spend their workdays in the field calling on the key accounts.

The Sales Process

The following chapters will discuss the eight steps of the sales process: prospecting, preapproach, approach, need identification, presentation, handling objections, gaining commitment, and follow-up. These steps are shown in Figure 1-3, the Sales Process. As previously noted, when utilizing a traditional selling method, the salesperson spends little time on the early stages of the process—especially the approach and need identification. Therefore, the typical prospect may not be properly qualified or is not convinced that he or she needs the product or service; so gaining commitment, or closing the sale, becomes very difficult, tedious, and time-consuming for the salesperson. However, under a consultative approach, much more time is devoted to the early stages of the sales process, specifically prospecting, preapproach, approach, and need identification. As a result, gaining commitment from the prospect becomes a very natural, logical next step. Ideally, the salesperson has defined the customer's needs and has clearly linked them to the benefits offered by the product or service; thus, the customer is readily convinced that the product/service will solve his or her problem or meet a need. Having needs met, whether they be latent (for example, image or status) or manifest (such as, need for meeting space), is the reason behind every purchase made.

Key Concepts

In Chapter 1, the following key concepts have been discussed:

- Personal selling offers several advantages: salespersons can adapt their presentations to suit the needs of individual customers, immediate feedback from the customer can be responded to during sales presentations, and the effectiveness of personal selling can be more easily measured. Personal selling also drives the revenues of the organization.
- Personal selling involves direct communication with a prospective customer in order to develop a relationship, identify customer needs, match goods/services with those needs, communicate benefits to customers, and gain commitment to purchase goods/services that satisfy customer needs. The definition is aligned with the consultative sales approach.
- In the traditional selling method, little time is spent on the early stages of the process, so closing a sale is awkward and difficult. In the consultative sales method, a great deal of time is spent in the early stages so that commitment is gained as a very natural, or logical, next step.

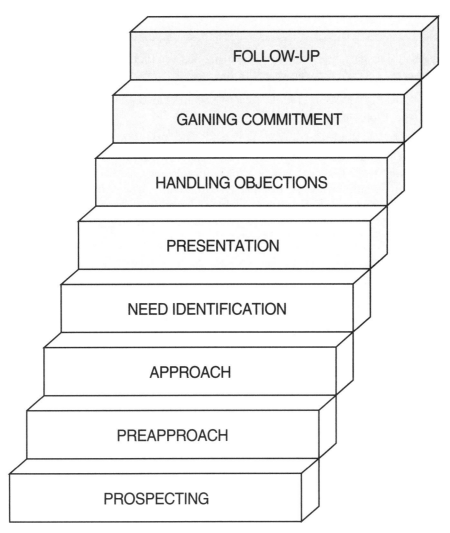

Figure 1-3 The Sales Process

- The common characteristics of good salespeople are described. In particular, the traits of adaptive selling, learning orientation, and customer orientation are highlighted.
- The sales process is composed of eight basic steps: prospecting, preapproach and planning, approaching the client, identifying client needs, presenting the product, handling objections, gaining commitment, and following up on and keeping promises.

Following this introductory chapter, each subsequent chapter will focus on a part of the sales process from prospecting through follow-up. In addition, chapters on contracts, servicing the customer, revenue management, and time management are included.

Endnotes

[1] To learn more about strategic sales planning, see Heiman, Stephen E., Diane Sanchez with Tad Tuleja (1998) *The New Strategic Selling*, New York: Warner Books, Inc.

[2] Spiro, Rosann L. and Barton A. Weitz (1990), "Adaptive Selling: Conceptualization, Measurement and Nomological Validity," *Journal of Marketing Research* 27 (February), 61-69.

[3] For more on learning orientation, see for example, Colquitt, Jason A. and Marcia J. Simmering (1998), "Conscientiousness, Goal Orientation, and Motivation to Learn During the Learning Process: A Longitudinal Study," *Journal of Applied Psychology* 83 (August), 654-665; Calantone, Roger J., S. Tamer Cavusgil, and Yushan Zhao, "Learning Orientation, Firm Innovation Capability, and Firm Performance," *Industrial Marketing Management* 31 (September), 515-524 and Celuch, Kevin G., Chickery J. Kasouf, and Venkatakrishnan Peruvemba (2002), "The Effects of Perceived Market and Learning Orientation on Assessed Organizational Capabilities," *Industrial Marketing Management* 31 (September), 545-554.

[4] Saxe, Robert and Barton A. Weitz (1982), "The SOCO Scale: A Measure of the Customer Orientation of Salespeople," *Journal of Marketing Research* 19 (August), 343-351.

[5] Weitz, Barton A., Sujan and Sujan (1986), "Knowledge, Motivation, and Adaptive Behavior: A Framework for Improving Selling Effectiveness," *Journal of Marketing* 50 (October), 174-191; Grewal, Dhruv and Arun Sharma (1991), "The Effect of Salesforce Behavior on Customer Satisfaction: An Interactive Framework," *Journal of Personal Selling & Sales Management* 11 (Summer), 13- 23; Goolsby, Jerry R., Rosemary R. Lagace, and Michael L. Boorom (1992), "Psychological Adaptiveness and Sales Performance," *Journal of Personal Selling & Sales Management* 12 (Spring), 51-66; Deshpandé, Rohit, John U. Farley, and Frederick E. Webster (1993), "Corporate Culture, Customer Orientation, and Innovativeness in Japanese Firms: A Quadrad Analysis," *Journal of Marketing* 57 (January), 23-27; Williams, Michael R. and Jill S. Attaway (1996), "Exploring Salespersons' Customer Orientation as a Mediator of Organizational Culture's Influence on Buyer-Seller Relationships," *Journal of Personal Selling & Sales Management* 16 (Fall), 33-52.

[6] For more information on the various sales office roles, see Ismail, Ahmed (1999), *Hotel Sales & Operations*, Albany: Delmar Publishers.

[7] Kotler, Philip, John Bowen, and James Makens, (2003), *Marketing for Hospitality and Tourism*, 3rd ed., Upper Saddle River, NJ: Prentice Hall.

Prospecting and Preapproach

his chapter discusses the prospecting and preapproach stages of the sales process. The chapter begins by examining the various meetings market segments that frequently play a crucial role in the livelihood of hospitality firms. Next, the importance of prospecting and present popular methods of identifying prospective customers are discussing the chapter ends by investigating the preapproach stage and providing suggestions for collecting precall data.

Meetings Market Segments

There are a number of market segments that are related to the hospitality industry. Each of these segments, and the groups contained within, are different and it is incorrect to stereotype specific types of groups. However, some broad generalizations about each group market segment can be made. According to *Successful Meetings*, the meetings market is estimated at $141.3 billion in total expenditures for 2003.[1] Table 2-1 provides a breakdown of the meetings market by the three main categories: meetings, association conventions, and corporate meetings. It is interesting to note that corporations account for the largest number of meetings while attendees of associations and conventions account for more in total expenditures. The reason for this will become clear after reading the following sections.

Table 2-1: 2001 Meetings Market

	Corporate	Convention	Association	Total
Number of Meetings (in thousands)	844.1	11.8	177.7	1033.6
Expenditures (in billions)	$10.3	$16.6	$13.9	$40.8
Number of attendees (in millions)	51.5	12.5	15.9	79.9

Source: Braley, Sarah J. F., editor. 2002. "Overview." *Meetings & Conventions*, (August): 3-42.

Association Market Segment. The association market is very broad, ranging from large national and international conventions attended by thousands of individuals to very small, but expensive, board of directors' meetings. The association market tends to be thought of as large conventions, but this is only a small segment of the total associations meeting market. Associations hold several different types of meetings each year, including the following:

- **Annual convention for the entire membership**. This is usually the largest meeting that the association will hold. It will often include exhibits, especially within the trade association market.
- **Board of directors' meetings**. These are typically held three or four times a year and are often quite elaborate. The expenditures per attendee are higher than for other association meetings.
- **Seminars and workshops**. Associations provide continuing education for the members at meetings held throughout the year.
- **Committee meetings**. Associations operate by means of the volunteer committee approach and each of the committees may need to meet several times a year.

The decision-making process and *long* lead time for the association market can be frustrating for the hospitality sales manager. This market segment is often assigned to the most experienced sales manager or the director of sales because that individual's additional experience will prove beneficial in working with the association market segment. The meeting planners working with the larger associations are normally quite experienced and professional, so the property's representative must be equally knowledgeable and experienced. The decision-making is scattered among several people within the association. For example, the meeting planner may make the decision concerning where to hold small meetings and workshops, but decisions about larger meetings, such as annual conventions, normally involve the executive committee and/or the board of directors. For this reason, the sales manager must be prepared for a lengthy decision-making process. The initial contact may be with the association meeting planner, but it may take several weeks or months before the board of directors makes a final decision concerning the location for a large meeting.

The lead time for planning meetings can also be quite long. For the largest of the national associations, it is common for the site of the annual convention to be selected five to ten years in advance. Even smaller associations typically plan their annual conventions one to three years in advance. This lead time creates some real challenges for the sales and marketing staff. Even if a large annual meeting is booked now, the revenue will not be realized for quite some time in the future.

Associations often use the annual convention as a revenue-producing event, where the revenue is then used to fund some of the association's annual operating expenses. For this reason, associations will be sensitive about such negotiable items as meeting room rental, complimentary room policies, food and beverage prices, and, in some cases, room rates. Keep in mind that association attendees will be paying their own expenses to attend meetings and may be very sensitive about prices for guest rooms, suites, food, and beverages.

Another popular member of the association market is the **SMERF** group. SMERF is an acronym that stands for a combination of several market segments–social, military, educational, religious, and fraternal. SMERF meetings are frequently held in conjunction with nonprofit groups that are often working with a very limited budget. They usually do not have a professional meeting planner. While some of the SMERF meetings are small, the number of meetings that the SMERF market segment generates makes the overall contribution significant.

Corporate Market Segment. This market segment is very broad and is widely solicited by hotels. The corporate market is quite different from the association market segment. The differences include needs and objectives, the type and number of individuals in attendance, and the lead time required. Corporations hold many more meetings than associations. The meetings tend to be smaller, have a much shorter lead time, are less price sensitive, are subject to quicker site decisions, and involve fewer individuals in the decision-making process.

Corporate meetings are attractive to hospitality organizations for several reasons. They are held throughout the year rather than being concentrated in certain periods or months, and they do not require as extensive a use of meeting rooms as the association market segment. The typical corporation meeting involves fewer than 50 attendees. The types of corporate meetings vary widely, including the following:

- **Training meetings**. With the advent of new technology, corporations are always holding meetings to train new staff and provide update training for current staff. This type of meeting is perhaps the most common. Many hospitality firms located near the offices of major corporations will solicit this type of meeting on a continual basis.

- **Sales meetings**. Most corporations maintain a sales staff that meets on a frequent basis. These meetings serve both to provide information to the sales staff and to motivate them. The sales meeting is an excellent type of meeting to solicit because the group is normally less concerned about price than are other types of meetings groups. The organization is concerned about providing attendees with convenience and comfort.

- **New product introduction meetings**. When a corporation introduces a new product, it is often done with great fanfare. The meeting is likely to be attended by dealers, corporate sales staff, and the media. This type of meeting can be very extensive and very price insensitive.

- **Management meetings**. Management staff members often need to "get away" from the place of business to meet and discuss issues in a quiet environment, where they will not be interrupted by telephones and other office distractions.

- **Technical meetings**. Technical specialists need to meet to discuss items of mutual concern. This type of meeting is less elaborate than the other types of corporate meetings.

- **Annual stockholders' meeting**. All publicly held corporations are required to have annual stockholders' meetings that may be attended by a large number of individuals. Some food and beverage events associated with stockholders' meetings can be very extensive.

- **Board of directors' meetings**. These are perhaps the most elaborate and expensive, and often feature extensive food and beverage presentations. They also require more expensive and specialized meeting rooms.

Meeting planning within corporations is typically spread among several departments. The larger corporations that tend to have many meetings have established meeting planning departments. However, in most corporations, meetings are planned by people with other areas of responsibility, such as marketing or human resources, or independent planners are used. The decision-making is usually rapid and does not involve as many individuals as does the association market. If the meeting planner is not the final decision-maker, the planner is usually highly influential in the decision-making process.

In addition to business meetings, corporations also plan **incentive meetings or trips** for their employees as a reward for outstanding performance. Incentive meetings tend to be held at resort properties in exotic locations and aboard cruise lines. In many ways, incentive meetings are similar to association meetings in that location and climate are very important, and there is an emphasis on recreation and relaxation. Also, attendance is voluntary, spouses often attend, and the trips must be heavily promoted to encourage employees to perform well in hopes of "winning" a place on the trip. The lead time for planning incentive trips is a year or more, they last four to five days on average, and they can be attended by anywhere from 10 to 1,000 people (the average is approximately 100). Business meetings are normally scheduled for tax purposes (so participants do not have to report trips as taxable income), but they are often canceled or ignored by the meeting attendees. However, incentive trips do resemble corporate meetings in that the decision-making is centralized, a master account is used for billing, service is important, planners are not price sensitive, and there are established guarantees for rooms and meals.

Decision Factors. The association and corporate markets are natural segments for the group business market because of their clear distinctions in meeting characteristics. In addition, sales managers need to understand the factors that are important to each buyer in selecting a facility. Table 2-2 contains a comparison of the rankings of the factors considered important to buyers for the types of meetings.

Table 2-2: Ranking of Factors Considered Very Important in Selection of a Facility/Hotel

	Corporate	Convention	Association
Quality of food service	1	3	4
Negotiable food, beverage, and room rates	2	2 (tie)	1
Number, size, and quality of meeting rooms	3	1	2
Cost of hotel or meeting facility	4	4	3
Efficiency of billing procedures	5	5	5
Meeting support services and equipment	6	6	8
Efficiency of check-in and check-out procedures	7	7	7
Number, size, and quality of sleeping rooms	8	2 (tie)	6
Assignment of one staff person to handle all aspects of meeting	9	8	9

Source: Braley, Sarah J.F., editor. 1998. "The Big Picture." *Meetings & Conventions* October: 19, 35; *Meetings & Conventions' 2002 Meetings Market Report.*

While it is important to deal with each buyer on an individual basis, the responses in the table from the average meeting planner will provide a place to start.

As the table shows, there are some differences in the factors that are most important for the various types of meetings. Corporate planners are most concerned about the quality of food, followed by the ability to negotiate rates and the number, size and quality of meeting rooms. Convention planners are most concerned about the number, size, and both quality of meeting rooms and sleeping rooms, and the ability to negotiate rates. Finally, association planners tend to be less in agreement as to the most important factors, but the ability to negotiate rates received the most 'very important' responses. These planners are also worried about the meeting rooms, quality of food, and the cost of the facilities. The top four in rank are the same for the three types of meetings, but the factors differ somewhat in importance. It should also be noted that convention planners placed importance on exhibit space, but it was not included due to the lack of importance among association and corporate planners.

The preceding discussion should assist in defining the broad market. However, within that market it is necessary to identify those individuals or organizations that have a need for a product or service. The following section focuses on finding prospects for a hospitality product.

Prospecting

The importance of prospecting and its contribution to the salesperson's success cannot be overstated. The salesperson must become—and stay—prospect minded. **Prospecting**, simply stated, is finding potential customers who have a need for a product or service, and who possess the ability and authority to purchase from the salesperson. Another term used for describing these customers is qualified sales leads. Regardless of how much business the salesperson has, he or she should devote some time each week—one-half to a full day—to prospecting.[2] Doing so will prevent the month-to-month income variation—the roller-coaster effect—often experienced by salespeople.

Prospects come from many sources. Utilize as many means of prospecting as possible, and build an extensive base of qualified sales leads. Only a small percentage of prospects will ever become actual customers. In general, overall business figures indicate that a salesperson has to make three to five sales calls to obtain one sale. In some industries, however, this ratio may be much higher. For example, in the insurance industry 10 to 25 sales calls are common to obtain one completed sale. For this reason, sales are often considered a "numbers game." The more prospects one has, the better the chances are to turn a portion of them into clients.

Methods of Prospecting

Many methods of prospecting exist. Indeed, you are likely using a variety of these methods with varying effectiveness in your present sales position. The following paragraphs will discuss a partial list of some of the more popular means of prospecting, which include the natural market, cold calling, referred leads, centers of influence, nests, repeat business, local organizations and companies, personal observation, conversing, and situation prospecting.

Natural Market

The **natural market** is made up of family, friends, and acquaintances. This market is created by anyone in a normal, natural, routine way. A salesperson should not hesitate to let members of his or her natural market know about the business. Also, they can be asked for any potential prospects they may hear of in their various work and social situations.

Cold Calls

Cold calls refer to contacting prospective customers without a prior appointment or announcement. Cold calling potential customers by telephone is usually conducted with the goal of securing a face-to-face appointment with the prospect. Face-to-face sales presentations are much more effective and this form of sales approach should be used whenever possible.

Cold calling also includes physically stopping by the business or home locations of prospects without a pre-arranged appointment. Although such face-to-face interaction is most effective, some prospects may have very strict guidelines regarding the times that salespeople are allowed to visit their business locations. Salespeople should adhere to these specified days and times.

Sales blitzes are cold calls designed to turn the sales force out en masse to telephone or visit as many potential customers as possible. Frequently, the goal of a sales blitz is to make prospects aware of a particular property or promotional offer, and to gather potential sales leads. This task may be accomplished by dropping off sales collateral and/or inexpensive gifts and conversing long enough to identify key decision makers and possible needs.

Cold calls typically make salespeople uncomfortable, but nearly all salespeople must make some cold calls at some point in their careers. To maximize cold calls, Robert Garvey of *Entrepreneur* offers this sales tip: "Set a goal to make 100 cold calls in 30 days without worrying about the results. By the end of 100 calls, you know your business intimately because you have fielded so many questions and objections to buying from so many people. This process also lifts your self-confidence quickly and without emotional stress because you haven't worried about selling. At the end of the 100 calls, you are ready to sell. You will make better calls on better people. You will know what to say when you go in.[3]

Referred Leads

Referred leads are predicated upon the theory that from each interview or each client a salesperson should be able to secure names of other prospects. Satisfied clients are excellent sources for leads, as are company employees who may come into contact with potential customers through church, sports leagues, or other associations. Casual contacts, such as real estate agents, bankers, and moving companies, are also good sources for referrals.

For example, one enterprising sales manager developed a contest in which all employees (front desk, bellmen, accountants, housekeeping, etc.) were asked to provide the names of business contacts to the sales department. Cash prizes were given to the employee who generated the most revenue-producing sales leads, the employee who submitted leads with the greatest future potential, the employee who identified the greatest number of new leads, and the employee who utilized the most creative method for generating leads. At the conclusion of the two-month-long contest, the sales department reaped more than $10,000 in incremental income from 162 leads generated by 38 employees.

The term **endless chain** describes the most effective use of referred leads. To employ this strategy, attempt to get from each person interviewed, information about and/or introductions to three of his or her acquaintances who may possess the need for the product and services.

Unfortunately, salespeople are often uncomfortable asking for referrals, although referrals are the best means of identifying sales leads. The most successful salespeople build their sales practices largely through referrals, and referrals are the most efficient means of producing new sales. Indeed, the data in financial services indicates that one sale is gained for every 3.3 referrals compared to every 10 seminar attendees, every 50 cold calls, or every 60 letters.[4]

Prior to asking for referrals, the salesperson should ensure that the customer is satisfied, even if a sale has not been completed. If the customer is pleased with the process, the salesperson should not hesitate to ask for a referral. Referred leads have many benefits, including shorter sales cycles, faster closings, and larger initial transactions, so asking for referrals should be a standard part of the salesperson's sales presentation. Few salespeople, however, ask for referred leads, so they miss the best opportunity to develop a strong network of clients. If you are reluctant to ask for referrals, note that more than 80 percent of customers report they would gladly provide referrals if asked.[5]

Practice asking for referrals with friends. (See Figure 2-1, How to Ask for Referrals.) Referred leads are an important source of leads and the worst that can happen is that the customer will say no. (See Figure 2-2, Handling Objections When Prospecting for Referrals.) Also, think of other creative ways to gain referred leads. For example, one salesperson asks customers to provide a few names of prospects when they have time. He then leaves a brightly colored, stamped, self-addressed envelope and paper with customers. The bright colors serve as a reminder to customers and are not easily lost in a shuffle of papers on a desk. This salesperson estimates that he receives about a 30 percent response rate. Although he is not nearly attaining the proportion of 80 percent of customers that might respond to a more direct request, at least this salesperson is obtaining some useful referred leads. Remember, it is a volume game.

Centers of Influence

A **center of influence** is a person who can, and will, influence other people to give a salesperson an appointment to discuss their needs. Centers of influence have an unusual amount of prestige and influence with others, and they are persons to whom one can return for referred leads over a long period of time. For example, ministers, florists, and photographers serve as centers of influence for couples planning their weddings.

1. **Get the nominator to express an affirmative feeling.**

   This means getting the nominator—the person you want to help you identify possible prospects—to verbalize positive feelings about you or your service (e.g., "How do you feel about the process that we have been through? Has this been helpful?"). Ensure that your nominator is in a receptive, positive mood. Your ability to obtain referred leads depends on it.

2. **Suggest a name or give a category.**

   The objective is to help the nominator think of names (e.g., "I'd like to meet some other people like yourself, John/Mary; someone who helps plan special events for his or her organization. Can you think of any of your acquaintances in the area that might be involved in such planning?").

   Names and categories come from what you've learned about the nominator in preparation and during the interview. This step is inseparable from Step 1 and Step 3.

3. **Qualify the prospect in depth.**

   Qualifying means evaluating the prospects. Know which questions are important in your process. Ask the qualifying questions in the same order each time (e.g., "Tell me about Joe. For whom does he work? What exactly does he do there?"). Gain knowledge about the prospect's business, markets, and personality.

4. **Ask who else came to mind while describing the prospect.**

   Continue obtaining names by assuming there are other people (e.g., "Chances are, John/Mary, while you were thinking of Joe, some other names flashed through your mind. Tell me, who else came to mind?"). Always qualify people after asking "who else."

5. **Ask the nominator to identify the one person he or she knows well who has the best opportunity to rise to the top.**

   Pinpointing helps you focus on the best leads. Pinpointing helps you find out what makes that person special. Pinpointing helps build networks of guests.

Figure 2-1 How to Ask for Referrals

Nests

A **nest** is a group of people that is closely knit by reason of one or more relationships. The people making up a potential nest have one or more things in common. The relationship may be business, occupational, family, social, religious, or community.

1. **If your client can't think of anyone . . .**

   X   Suggest a name or a category

2. **If your client says, "I can't think of anyone who is in the market for hotel services . . ."**

   X   "I am not concerned with whether people are in the market for hotel services, I am concerned about having the ability to meet people just like you."

3. **If your client says, "I'd like to talk to them first."**

   X   "I think that is a great idea!"

   Describe your approach . . . "whether they want to meet with me is entirely up to them."

4. **If you encounter strong negativism,**

   X   "Sounds like you've had a bad experience."

   Listen *empathetically*. Obtain a positive response to your approach (professional, helpful, and beneficial) and describe how you plan to contact the referral.

Figure 2-2 Handling Objections When Prospecting for Referrals

For example, if the property is dealing with one department within a large corporation, there may be additional departments that could also use services. Thus, if the salesperson is working with the human resources department to provide meeting space for training employees, the salesperson might also find that the information technology group can use hotel services if it is involved in long-term installations that require bringing in specialists.

Repeat Business among Your Clientele

The majority of the sales made by highly successful salespeople come from **repeat business**, those guests with whom they have previously worked. It is advantageous for a salesperson to do everything possible to develop a strong and lasting relationship with those customers that were sold to earlier.

Local Organizations and Companies

Local organizations and companies may be large sources of business, especially for out-of-town visitors and home office personnel. Make a point to visit each identified business and introduce yourself for future reference. To encourage patronage, consider inviting key personnel from each of these businesses and organizations to a reception. Also, participate in local organizations like the Rotary Club, Jaycees, and the Chamber of Commerce. Remember: Friends do business with friends.

Other Prospecting Techniques

In addition to the more formal prospecting sources, there are three informal techniques that a salesperson will find helpful.

Personal Observation

Many clients will simply evolve if you stay aware and alert to situations taking place around you. Follow the media to identify companies moving to your area and to stay knowledgeable regarding news of existing companies, such as expansions or new contracts. Remaining alert and being aware of changes taking place around you will allow you to add a substantial number of potential prospects to your list.

Conversing

As is often the case in the process of interviewing a potential customer, the initial conversation will be largely small talk. During this time the salesperson is afforded the opportunity to discuss or listen for the names of people that could be potential referred leads. In other words, be a good listener.

As an example, "I see, Bill, that you are on the Board of XYZ company. Who serves on that Board with you?" "I notice, Dorothy, there is a new business down the street. Can you tell me who is the owner of that business?" Following the interview, make a note of those names so you can call on them as a form of a referred lead.

Situation Prospecting

People often buy products because a change has taken place that suggests a need for the product or service sold. Situation prospecting concentrates effort on asking for situations rather than asking for names of individuals. As an example, "Mary, of your acquaintances or business associates, have any recently gone into business for him- or herself?"

Prospecting Exercise

As the preceding discussion illustrates, prospects can be obtained in a variety of ways. You are only limited by your degree of creativity. In the following prospecting exercise, taking 5 minutes to identify other sources or methods for prospecting. Do some brainstorming and let your creative juices flow.

_____

_____

_____

_____

_____

_____

_____

_____

_____

_____

_____

_____

_____

_____

_____

_____

_____

Build and Upgrade Clientele

In addition to where and how buyers are found, a salesperson needs to know how to build and upgrade clientele. First, identify the target market of your particular company. Should you be seeking to identify prospective business travelers, associations, vacationers, or conventioneers? If business travelers are the primary market of your firm, are you interested in attracting small businesses, professional practices, divisions of large corporations, or large multinational corporations? The more precise you are about what comprises your target market, the better job you can do at building your client base.

Building a clientele provides a salesperson with a continuous and adequate supply of high-grade probable buyers. Professional sales representatives regard their prospect file in the same light as they regard their personal bank account. They know that they must make regular deposits to offset withdrawals. If they fail to do this, they know that their prospect account will soon become bankrupt.

Preapproach

To effectively conduct business with prospects, so that both your time and the prospects' time are well spent, you must know and understand the prospects and their respective businesses. In other words, you should research the prospects and their companies so that you have all the available facts before meeting with the prospect. An executive vice president of a large company, for example, becomes very irritated with salespeople who question him about information that is readily available on the company's web site. This executive feels that such salespeople are wasting his time and he refuses to do business with them.

The information you need to conduct a strong sales interview and presentation is often available on the Internet, in annual reports, in company brochures, and in news items. Other information may be obtained by calling or visiting the company's office and speaking to the receptionist or the secretary of the decision-maker you hope to see. You can simply explain that you are seeking information that will help you develop a rapport with Mr./Ms. Doe, and that you would appreciate any information the receptionist can provide. Always ask, "Can you please help me?" In other words, work to qualify the prospect by determining if there is a need for your product/service and whether the prospect is the decision-maker. Let prospects know that you are serious about gaining their business by doing your homework!

Prior to calling on clients there are some questions that you should try to answer regarding prospects and their respective firms. While this list is fairly extensive, your goal should be to learn as many facts about the prospects and their companies as possible, prior to your sales presentation.

- What is the prospect's business or association?
- What is it that the prospect's company does?
- Where does the firm operate?
- Who are the key decision-makers in the prospect's firm?
- What are the company's geographical patterns or limitations?
- Who are the major competitors of the prospect's firm?
- What major trends are occurring in the prospect's particular industry?
- Does the prospect's company use hospitality services? When and how often?
- What is important to the prospect's decision-makers when selecting a particular hospitality service?
- With whom does the prospect's company do business for hospitality services and why?
- Who is responsible for preparing meeting and event budgets? Who approves these budgets?
- What is the company's time cycle for meetings and other events?

- What is the company's lead time for meetings and other events?
- What kind of attendance is expected at company meetings or events?
- What is the typical duration of a company meeting or event?

In addition to questions about the prospect's business, it is helpful to obtain personal information about the prospect, which may assist you in rapidly developing a rapport through common interests. Consequently, you may want to know:

- Is the prospect married? If yes, what is the spouse's name?
- Does the prospect have children?
- What college did the prospect attend?
- What are the prospect's hobbies?

 # Preapproach Exercise

The more information you know about your prospect, the better your ability to develop rapport and to tailor your sales presentation. In the following preapproach exercise, take a few minutes to identify key pieces of information, other than those previously discussed, that should be obtained prior to making your initial sales presentation.

_____

_____

_____

_____

_____

_____

_____

_____

_____

_____

_____

_____

Customer Mapping

As many researchers have noted, one way salespeople can be substantively more effective is by mapping out the buying roles of their prospects.[6] Essentially, in any sale there are four customer roles involved. In complex sales, one or more persons may serve in each role, while in more simple sales, one person may serve in several roles. The customer roles include:

- **Final Decision-maker.** This person has the *final* say regarding the decision to buy, and may veto the sale even when all others have said yes or may approve the sale when all others have said no. This individual has the ability to release the funds to complete the sale.

- **User.** This individual will use or supervise the use of your product or service. This person's success is often tied to how well your product or service works. Hence, the user will be judging your product/service based on how much it will enhance his or her performance or status.

- **Influencer.** This individual sets specifications and therefore pares down or eliminates the list of potential suppliers. The influencer will base the recommendations on how well the product or service meets the specifications. Although the influencer cannot approve the purchase of your product or service, he or she can give a final veto. Beware, sometimes influencers believe they are the final decision-makers when they are not. You should ask enough questions to ensure that you have identified the final decision-maker.

- **Mentor.** The mentor provides information and advises you as to how you might best obtain the sale. The mentor is someone who can benefit in some way by your gaining the sale. Thus, the mentor will provide guidance regarding the people who will be most influential in determining the success of the sale. The mentor must be someone who believes in you and your product/service, and has a great deal of credibility with the buying organization.

It is critical to identify and understand the people who fill each of these roles as you move into the sales process. You should make personal contact with each individual who performs these roles, or arrange to have someone else from your firm make the contact.

Customer Mapping Exercise

Think about one account with which you are working. On the following chart, identify the individuals who fit each role. Next, estimate the degree of influence (high, medium, or low) that you believe each of these individuals holds in determining the success of your sale. Finally, assess the degree (strong, neutral, or weak) to which you have developed a relationship with that individual. If you do not know the individual(s) who fills each of these buying roles and the amount of influence they control, you should recognize this as a red flag—meaning your position with regard to selling this account is weak.[7]

Final Decision-Maker						User				
Name	Degree of Influence	Relationship	Change Receptivity	Rating		Name	Degree of Influence	Relationship	Change Receptivity	Rating

Influence						Mentor				
Name	Degree of Influence	Relationship	Change Receptivity	Rating		Name	Degree of Influence	Relationship	Change Receptivity	Rating

Buyers' Receptivity to Change

As part of the analysis of prospects, a salesperson should also evaluate the prospective buyers' degree of satisfaction with their supplier of the product or service, as well as their satisfaction with their own business performance. When prospects recognize a gap between where they are and where they want to be, they are more receptive to change. Thus, they will be more receptive to a new product or service that will help them eliminate that gap. As a result, a salesperson will have a better chance of obtaining an appointment and closing a sale with these prospects.[8]

When the gap is small, the buyer is open to suggestions for improvement, but may not be actively seeking new solutions (*Dissatisfied*). The larger the gap, the more urgent the buyer's need to find a solution for closing that gap (*Threatened*). The threatened buyer is likely seeking new solutions and will need answers in a hurry. Conversely, when buyers believe they are doing as well as they can be (*Complacent*) or believe they are doing better than they thought they would be (*Smug*), they will be unreceptive to change. Hence, the ability to sell to these buyers is quite low, unless the salesperson can convince them that there is a threat to their current position on the horizon.

You should seek to identify your prospects' willingness to change early in the sales interview. Although you do not want to completely discount the buyers who are less receptive to change, you should focus on those prospects falling into the dissatisfied or threatened categories. You will find the sales process can be completed more rapidly with prospects in these two groups. You should, however, remain in routine, but not too frequent, contact with those prospects who fall into the smug or complacent categories, as their situations may change. Your prior acquaintance and perseverance may provide you with an advantage in eventually obtaining these accounts.

Change Receptivity Exercise

Go back to your customer-mapping chart from the previous exercise. Try to identify where each buyer stands in regard to change. Is the buyer recognizing a need for improvement? How strong is that need? Is the buyer merely **dissatisfied** or **threatened**? Is the buyer happy where he or she is? Is he or she **complacent** or **smug**?

After determining each customer's receptivity to change, rate each buyer on how he or she feels about your product/service using the following nine-point scale:

9 = extremely enthusiastic supporter

8 = strongly supportive

7 = moderately supportive

6 = slightly supportive

5 = disinterested

4 = slightly negative

3 = moderately negative

2 = strongly negative

1 = extremely strong adversary

If you do not know where each buyer stands in regard to change, or if you do not know how each buyer feels about your product/service, you should "red flag" the buyer. Until you have definitely learned otherwise, red-flagged buyers should be considered extremely strong adversaries.

Re-examine your customer-mapping chart again to be sure no inconsistencies exist. Are your change receptivity classifications (dissatisfied, threatened, complacent, smug) consistent with your ratings of how each buyer feels about your product/service?[9]

Key Concepts

Chapter 2 has focused on prospecting and preapproach. The key points of this chapter include:

- The three primary market segments within the hospitality industry are association meetings, conventions, and corporate meetings. Corporate meetings account for the greatest number of meetings, while conventions account for the largest meeting expenditures.
- Prospecting is finding potential customers who have a need for a product or service, and who possess the ability and authority to purchase from the salesperson.
- Methods of prospecting include the natural market, cold calling, referred leads, centers of influence, nests, repeat business, local organizations and companies, personal observation, conversing, and situation prospecting. Using referred leads is the most effective method of prospecting.
- Preapproach involves researching prospects and their companies, so the salesperson should have all available facts before making the sales presentation. Do your homework!
- Utilize customer mapping as a strategy to ensure that all those individuals that may be involved in the purchase decision have effectively been reached. If you cannot identify the final decision-maker, user, influencer, and mentor for each of your accounts, you should proceed with caution.
- Customer mapping is used to identify the degree of influence and receptivity to change that each individual involved in the decision process holds. In addition, customer mapping encourages the salesperson to assess the strength of the relationship that he or she has with each of these individuals.

Endnotes

[1] See Anonymous, "Meetings Market Outlook: Size of the Market," www.successmtgs.com/successmtgs/images/pdf/sm_market%20overview.pdf.

[2] Heiman, Stephen E., Diane Sanchez with Tad Tuleja (1998), *The New Strategic Selling*, New York: Warner Books.

[3] McGarvey, Robert (1995), "Listen Up!" *Entrepreneur*, August, 104-110.

[4] Patrick Leone (2002), "The Right Way to Get Referrals," *Advisor Today* (October): 84.

[5] Lorge, Sarah (1998), "Selling101: The Best Way to Prospect," *Sales and Marketing Management* (January), 80.

[6] For detailed information on buying center research see Heiman, Stephen E., Diane Sanchez with Tad Tuleja (1998) *The New Strategic Selling*, New York: Warner Books; Johnston, Wesley J. and Jeffrey E. Lewin, "Organizational Buying Behavior: Toward an Integrative Framework," *Journal of Business Research* 35 (January 1996), 1-15; Lichtenthal, J. David (1988), "Group Decision Making in Organizational Buying: A Role Structure Approach," in *Advances in Business Marketing*, vol. 3, ed. Arch G. Woodside (Greenwich, CT: JAI Press), 119-157; Webster, Frederick E., Jr. and Yoram Wind (1972), *Organizational Buying Behavior*, Englewood Cliffs, NJ: Prentice-Hall.

[7] For more information on customer mapping, see Heiman, Stephen E., Diane Sanchez with Tad Tuleja (1998) *The New Strategic Selling*, New York: Warner Books; Lilien, Gary L. and M. Anthony Wong (1984), "Exploratory Investigation of the Structure of the Buying Center in the Metalworking Industry," *Journal of Marketing Research* 21 (February), 1-11; Woodside, Arch G. (1992), "Conclusions on Mapping How Industry Buys," in *Advances in Business Marketing and Purchasing*, vol. 5 ed. Arch G. Woodside (Greenwich, CT; JAI Press, 1992), 283-300.

[8] For more information on buyer's responsiveness to change, see Heiman, Stephen E., Diane Sanchez with Tad Tuleja (1998) *The New Strategic Selling*, New York: Warner Books; McQuiston, Daniel H. and Peter R. Dickson (1991), "The Effect of Perceived Personal Consequences on Participation and Influence in Organizational Buying," *Journal of Business Research* 23 (September), 159-177.

[9] For a more detailed discussion of a buyer's willingness to change, see Heiman, Stephen E., Diane Sanchez with Tad Tuleja (1998) *The New Strategic Selling*, New York: Warner Books; Sheth, Jagdish N. (1973), "A Model of Industrial Buyer Behavior," *Journal of Marketing*, 37 (October), 50–56; Sheth, Jagdish N. (1996), "Organizational Buying Behavior: Past Performance and Future Expectations," *Journal of Business and Industrial Marketing* 11, 3/4 7-24.

APPROACH BY ADAPTING SOCIAL STYLE

he next two chapters explore the approach stage of the sales process, which facilitates development of a rapport with the buyer. This chapter begins by explaining the importance of identifying and adapting to the social styles of customers and follows with effective strategies for coping with each social style and customizing the sales presentation as necessary.

Social Styles

A key success factor in personal selling is **adaptive selling**, which means responding to customer needs by altering the content approach of the sales presentation.[1] That is, adaptive selling is the ability to use different sales approaches in different situations, and the ability to alter the sales approach based on a reassessment during the sales situation. Salespeople possessing adaptive skills are able to develop a rapport with a wide variety of customers and deal effectively with a diversity of sales situations.

Knowledge about customers and the selling situation are key to effective adaptation. To use this knowledge effectively, the wise salesperson categorizes information about customers by using the social style grid, as shown in Figure 3-1. This highly useful categorization method was initially created by

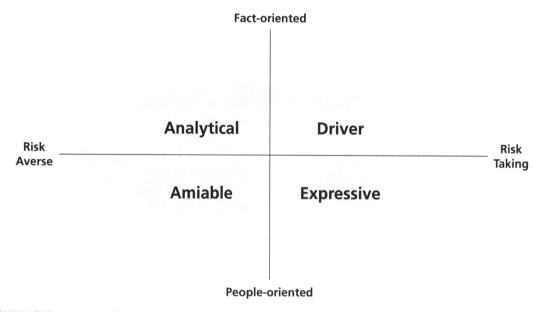

Figure 3-1 Social Style Grid—Social Styles Based on Behavioral Characteristics
Source: Adapted from Merrill, David and Reid, Roger (1981). *Personal Styles and Effective Performance:* Make Your Style Work for You. Radnor, PA: Chilton.

David Merrill and Roger Reid.[2] By using this grid, you can recognize the most effective method of communicating with the customer and define the best approach for a sales presentation.

Table 3-1: Characteristics Associated with the Social Styles

	Effective Application
Amiable Style	conceptual original imaginative creative broad-gauged idealistic intellectually tenacious ideological fact-oriented
Analytical Style	deliberative prudent weighs alternatives stabilizing objective rational analytical exact and precise
Expressive Style	people-oriented spontaneous persuasive empathetic grasps traditional values introspective draws out feelings of others loving informal
Driver Styles	action-oriented pragmatic assertive, directional results-oriented technically skillful objective (base opinions on what is actually seen) decisive bottom-line focus

It is important to recognize that social styles are not gender-specific and no one social style is better than another. Each social style has its good attributes. It is the job of the salesperson to recognize the social style of the customer and to adapt his or her own social style to the preferred communication style of the customer. That is, salespeople must routinely change how they communicate so that they are communicating with each individual prospect as though they share a common social style with the prospect. The most effective consultants and salespeople rarely claim, "I have a winning style." They think not in terms of a single selling style to suit all types of customers, but in terms of developing and using a repertoire of different selling styles to suit different customer types, needs, and styles. They not only sell themselves and their products or services; they sell their prospect. In the following sections, each of the social styles is described in some detail, and suggestions are given on how to both recognize and communicate with individuals who follow each social style.

Amiable Type

Overview. The amiable type is a visionary who places high value on ideas, innovations, concepts, theories, and long-range thinking. "Amiables" tend to derive their greatest satisfaction from the world of possibilities. In essence, amiables tend to be somewhat more stimulated and personally rewarded by efforts in problem-solving, rather than in implementing solutions. They often reveal an excellent imagination. Amiables tend to question themselves and others. They are not, therefore, accustomed to taking things for granted. They often seem to have an uncanny ability to anticipate or to project—to "know" prior to many others' knowing. Amiables usually resent being placed in situations where they are, in any sense, "hemmed in" or required to think or operate in a structured, well-defined manner. Amiables enjoy creating their own structure out of disorder; they excel in integrative tasks and situations demanding a long-term view.

amiables tend to be inward looking. That is, they enjoy drawing meaning from imagination. What they see and know to be most real is frequently seen by others as unreal and often "impractical." However, amiables' imaginative input serves as a catalyst for the thinking of those around them. Amiables are future-oriented and are typically less interested in what has been done in the past. In essence, they tend to live and derive satisfaction in terms of the future.

amiables are interested in developing personal relationships with others. These relationships are sought to reduce the risk amiables feel when required to make decisions. That is, amiables feel that a person who is a friend will not misdirect them, so they will be able to depend on this "friend" to provide accurate information and to assist them in the decision-making process. Because of the amiables' interest in people and relationships, the amiable generally dislikes conflict, and is very interested in ensuring that everyone is in consensus prior to making a decision.

When amiables are at their best, they will be seen as leaders and visionaries—they can cut through the smoke screens of tradition or past practices and focus on the crux of the situation. They are usually able to see profitable new directions or solutions of great value that others have missed. The amiable frequently brings up fresh and novel approaches and ideas. At their worst, amiables may be seen as "long on vision; short on action." amiables are individuals who may avoid some of the tedious nitty-gritty, and are not always comfortable making decisions. Often, they must be so convinced of the power and value of their insights and contributions that they may not see the necessity of documenting or detailing these contributions to the satisfaction of others. Indeed, at times, the amiable may seem quite impatient and irritated with others who demand detailed evidence or do not see the value of his or her ideas as he or she does.

Among amiable types we frequently find scientists, researchers, artists, professors, writers, corporate planners, and good "idea people." In community life, the amiable often may be encountered playing active roles on boards, task forces, planning committees, or agency leadership groups. Regardless of his or her job, a person who extensively employs the amiable style is stimulated by intellectual and creative problem-solving endeavors.

Initial Contact. When attempting to first establish contact with an amiable, write a letter to the amiable emphasizing your reliability, experience, and the quality of your service or product. Follow up with a phone call. The amiable may also be amenable to "cold" telephone contact. The amiable's secretary may ask for identification, but will not screen intensively. For openers with the amiable, you should use a referral by an acquaintance or you should pinpoint a researched need. If the amiable is busy, he or she may suggest calling you back or that you make an appointment with the secretary for a meeting. If the amiable accepts the phone call, the amiable may not be especially time-conscious. The amiable may be apt to consume your time in expansive conversation, but be difficult to pin down to practical, specific details that help you advance the sale. Amiables are often soft-spoken, so be prepared to speak more softly. Come across as friendly, candid, and casual.

Recognizing the amiable. The Amiable may have his or her secretary show you in, and be waiting for you, but appear preoccupied. If the amiable is concerned with surroundings, the office may be imaginative—decorated with new-wave furnishings and décor, including abstract paintings. If unconcerned, the office may be relatively unadorned. Futuristic books (e.g., science fiction) and periodicals may be handy. There may be citations for idealistic works—community service or other causes. The amiable may not be especially well organized.

As in other areas, the amiable's manner of dress may be hard to predict. The amiable may look like the absent-minded professor, caring little for clothes or the manner in which he or she presents him or herself. Also, the amiable may have an imaginative self-concept that leads to creation of his or her own style which, depending on his or her taste, may range from stunning to outlandish.

Sales Strategies for the amiable. The Amiable is intellectually interested, and responds well to research. If the amiable has had work published, you should be familiar with what writing exists, and what it is about. Learn the amiable's interests both in and out of business and attempt to familiarize yourself with them. The amiable may not expect you to be conversant about his or her interests, but would welcome acknowledgment that you know of them.

The amiable is most responsive to low-pressure, factual presentations combined with imaginative suggestions that may catch his or her fancy. Letters, reports and other messages play into his or her creativity and fascination with abstract concepts. On the other hand, the amiable welcomes not-too-detailed suggestions focused on practical concerns that he or she may not have the tolerance to spell out. The amiable is least responsive to minute, practical details, past history; and mundane present concerns.

In selling to an amiable, be well grounded in facts about your proposal; you should be able to relate it to the larger picture that may be proposed by your prospect. Offer the amiable a practical plan for accepting your proposal. Since the amiable may lack interest in practical matters, the amiable may not grasp their usefulness or how to implement them. Try to figure out the mundane detail work that will allow him or her to easily accept your proposal. Allow sufficient latitude for the amiable to toy with what you propose and how it may link to his or her own schemes. Ask for the amiable's opinion. Also, be prepared to find ties to practical concerns to expedite your proposal, since the amiable may very well spend the entire time on abstract matters, and may never get down to business. You may find it necessary to continue to guide the amiable back to your concerns, and—without frustrating or boring him or her—aim toward a practical conclusion. Be sure to state the benefits of your proposal.

When presenting to the amiable, watch for objections out of intolerance for detail. You may be called on to guide your prospect past these barriers and offer workable solutions that do not involve the amiable too heavily in minutia. If possible, find a subordinate of the amiable's with whom you can work out the minute details of your proposal. If the amiable's objections are substantive, prepare to support your contentions with data.

Also, look for means of tying your assertions to plans the amiable may have for future development. Offer enough data so that the amiable can draw favorable, substantive conclusions. As you become more familiar with the amiable's interests, look for new ways of likening your proposal to his or her future-oriented plans and needs. Finally, begin to give the amiable practical guidelines to follow. Set a comfortable deadline when you can make final arrangements; then, make those easy enough to deal with so that the amiable will not feel bogged down in detail. Remember, the amiable is not comfortable making decisions and will need both time and personal assurances from you. Assumptive closes are very effective with amiables. For a synthesis of the preceding discussion see Figure 3-2, Strategies for Dealing with the amiable.

Analytical Type

Overview. The **analytical** type is an individual who places high value on logic, ideas, and systematic inquiry. That is, the "analyticals" find satisfaction in identifying a problem, developing a variety of possible solutions, weighing them carefully, and testing them to see to it that the most logical systematic approach is followed. Consequently, analyticals are very "number-oriented."

Analyticals typically function in a steady, tenacious manner. Analyticals rely on their observations and rational principles while avoiding emotionalism and speculation. Analyticals often convey skepticism toward novel departures from what has been proven in the past—at least until such ideas or plans or programs have been thoroughly analyzed, tested, and reviewed in the light of other

Initial Contact

1. Send a personal letter. State who you are, why you are writing, your purpose in contacting the amiable. Stress your reputation, your reliability, your experience, the quality of your product and service, your follow through, your thoroughness.
2. Follow your letter with a personal phone call. Take time to be friendly, open, honest, sincere, and establish trust in the relationship.

Developing Rapport

1. Be on time.
2. Use time initially to establish the relationship.
3. Be prepared to share personal information about yourself.
4. Demonstrate that you are personally interested in the amiable.
5. Demonstrate that you want to understand the amiable's personal situation.
6. Feel free to engage in small talk before getting down to business.

Probing

1. Ask open-ended questions initially.
2. Make an effort to draw out the amiable's personal goals.
3. Ask how the amiable feels about the facts.
4. Listen responsively—give plenty of verbal/nonverbal feedback.
5. Ask "what," and "when" questions to clarify the amiable's goals.
6. Summarize the amiable's key concerns and feelings.

Presenting

1. Define clearly in writing what you will do to support the amiable's personal objectives.
2. Define what you and the amiable will need to contribute to reach the objectives.
3. Provide a clear solution to the amiable's problem(s).
4. Provide maximum guarantees and assurances that your solution will work in this case.
5. Show how your solution is best now and will be best in the future.
6. Explain features and benefits by telling "why."
7. Use third-party references wherever possible.

Figure 3-2 Strategies for Dealing with the amiable   (continues)

Closing

1. Ask for the order indirectly.
2. Don't push the amiable. Don't be overly assertive.
3. Emphasize guarantees and how the amiable is protected.
4. Don't corner the amiable. (Amiables want a way out if things go wrong.)
5. Get a commitment, even if it is based on a contingency.
6. Stress your personal involvement in follow-up services.
7. Try to avert the amiable's natural inclination to seek advice from others before signing.
8. Welcome objections and be patient and thorough in answering them.
9. Refer to experts wherever possible in third-party references.
10. Remember how the amiable feels and how he or she will be affected by the buying decision.

Figure 3-2 Strategies for Dealing with the amiable (continued)

possible alternatives. Analyticals are often quite skeptical of their own initial reactions and formulations as well as those of others. Therefore, analyticals frequently would rather "sleep on" a new idea and review it carefully before taking a position or making a commitment. Analyticals consciously avoid going off "half-cocked" or being swept along by the needs of the moment.

Analyticals very often are seen as consistent producers—logical "results getters" as opposed to people who are primarily visionaries or idea people. Thus, analyticals may often be valued for their prudence and thoughtful analysis rather than for their skill in mobilizing the enthusiasm of others. Analyticals are frequently sought out by others for the value of their objectivity and their cool thinking under pressure.

When analyticals are at their best, they may be seen as a consistent force for progress—topflight thinkers as well as doers. Analyticals will be seen as people who can cut through the smoke screens of untested ideas and emotional fervor. Frequently, analyticals can be highly effective in organizing themselves and others to research and plan. Hence, analyticals are of great assistance in executing logical, painstaking, and profitable projects.

At their worst, analyticals may be seen as rigid, overly cautious, and conservative—individuals who at times may emphasize deliberation to the de-emphasis of action. Analyticals may become so involved in weighing, testing, researching, and checking, that others perceive them as indecisive. Sometimes analyticals will be seen as stumbling blocks to actions that represent departures from tradition. When analyticals try to deal with change, basing actions on rational principles, analyticals may sometimes be viewed as rigid and dogmatic. For the aforementioned reasons, analyticals may be criticized for being mechanistic or impersonal. Often, at their worst, analyticals are accused of being overly cautious, overly methodical or overly logical. Sometimes people see analyticals as nonspontaneous or "dry" and "cold."

Analyticals typically tend to look at time from all dimensions—past, present, and future, which are seen as equally important. Analyticals typically are less concerned with making the so-called dramatic breakthrough than in correctly and consistently relating a present course of action to both the past and the future. Among analytical types are frequently found lawyers, engineers, scientists, technicians, professors, teachers, financially-oriented business personnel, systems analysts, electronic data processing specialists, and accountants.

Initial Contact. Initial contact with analyticals is best conducted through written communication. Compose a letter identifying your product, your expertise, and stressing the value of your product or service. Of all types, analyticals are least responsive to "cold" contact. Analyticals may suggest through a secretary that you write a letter outlining full details in a proposal, then pursue an orderly follow-up. If analyticals do take the phone, they may seem relatively distant. Analyticals may also ask particulars, seek proof for what you state, and ask for information on your product, company, and you. Analyticals will pin you down to facts and figures, and are inclined to make decisions based on data rather than personal contact. If you find this happening, your major task will be to interest analyticals in exploring data that you must present in person. Try to determine the kinds of information analyticals want; use that knowledge to generate face-to-face contact. Prepare a written proposal that presents the desired information in a step-by-step format. Remember, the analytical is most responsive to full documentation, well-organized statements of facts, supporting information, and elaboration of detailed plans. Analyticals are least responsive to puffery, pressure, vagueness, anecdotal material, inexact assertions, and nonsubstantive promotional generalities.

Recognizing the Analytical. Analyticals are inclined to formalities, and are very businesslike. Analyticals will be conservatively dressed—tailored and functionally neat. Analyticals will be prompt, and will have a secretary come and get you. Analyticals' businesslike surroundings are simple, perhaps sterile. Furnishings may be tasteful but conventional, and they are apt to have charts of business projects and other data displayed for easy use. Analyticals may have a considerable library of reports, reference works, data collections, government surveys, computer printouts, business studies, and comparison reports of his or her own and related businesses, but few human touches. The analytical's office and desk will be very orderly or neat, apt to contain files of data, computer printouts, and reference works. Of all types, Analyticals are most inclined toward recordkeeping.

Sales Strategies for the Analytical. Your analytical prospects may be inclined to formality and caution. Analyticals also may keep the interview at a fairly impersonal level. They do not want to be overwhelmed by pressure. Your best gambit is to offer the analytical as much background material and research data they want to see so that the they can draw their own conclusions. Analyticals will likely request fine details as a means of making comparisons with other proposals. You should provide well-organized, complete plans that include reasoned, sound suggestions for their implementation. Don't attempt to "snow" analyticals with tales of success or glowing reports of satisfied customers. Analyticals are not likely to jump on the bandwagon and may be put off by such tactics. You should strive to be precise in your discussion and to present factual alternatives.

Primarily, when selling to analyticals, let the facts speak for themselves. If the analyticals question your data, offer to research more. Make sure that analyticals know you understand the need for checking things out. If analyticals show you areas in which you cannot match the competition, you are better off admitting it than trying to make assertions you cannot prove. Analyticals will respect you more if you sharpen your plus items, and offer yours as a more advantageous total package. Watch for objections based on skepticism over vague sales points. Suggest contingency plans that will demonstrate your desire to give your best offer.

Let your proposal work for you in gaining analyticals' confidence, overcoming their caution and indecisiveness. When analyticals have reviewed enough facts and figures, and you sense that principal objections have been met, look to guide the sale toward a subliminal close. Suggest a "trial" test of your product/service so that the analyticals can conduct their own research. When the trial is complete, ask for the order directly. For a handy reference, see Strategies for Dealing with the Analytical in Figure 3–3.

Expressive Type

Overview. The expressive type places high value on human interaction. "Expressives" seek and enjoy the stimulation of contact with others and typically try to understand and analyze their own emotions and those of others. Expressives' concern for people, and understanding of them, usually makes them quite astute in "reading between the lines" about what people say and do.

Expressives are likely to be perceived as dynamic and stimulating. In particular, they are likely to be "warm" and closely in touch with others. Expressives are usually able to function in ways that demonstrate the ability to be sensitive to the needs and wants of others. Expressives are able to note discrepancies between speech and expression or between outward behavior and inner feeling. Expressives are sensitive to their own motives and those of others. For the aforementioned reasons, expressives often are seen as perceptive and insightful.

At their best, expressives are likely to be skilled in communication and patient, practical listeners and observers. They can often read and assess organizational politics with accuracy and insight. Expressives are people who can position and see change in ways that reduce resisting forces "before the fact" and thus increase the likelihood of cooperation, teamwork, and progress. Furthermore, expressives are frequently sought out for their ability to listen and empathize, and for their patience and forbearance in carrying assistance to others experiencing troubles or crises in their lives. At their worst, expressives may be seen as having much less interest in developing concepts, plans, or programs (or in systematically getting them to function) than they have in analyzing, communicating, and interpreting whatever is taking place. Many will see expressives as people who rely less on logic and thought than on "gut feel" or the way people and things emotionally "strike" them. Expressives seem to take their own emotional reactions, and what they infer that others feel, as representing "fact." Consequently, expressives frequently act on the basis of their feelings about things. Some may see expressives as defensive and over-reactive, and others may criticize expressives for subjectivity and emotionalism, which many may see as a substitute for action. Expressives may be perceived as intriguers who, in their well-intended efforts to draw others out, tend to fan latent emotional sparks

Initial Contact

1. Send a personal letter first. Provide specific product/service information, details about yourself, your company, your credentials as a technical expert. Stress how your product works, how it will be cost effective, your stability, your experience.
2. Follow letter with a phone call. Be businesslike, indicate the time you will need with the analytical, what you will bring to the meeting, how you will work with the analytical. Establish your competency based on your knowledge and technical expertise.

Developing Rapport

1. Be on time.
2. Show evidence that you have done your homework on the analytical's situation and possible needs.
3. Offer evidence of your problem-solving/analysis expertise.
4. Focus your attention on the analytical's needs.
5. Be deliberate.
6. Be ready to answer questions the analytical may have about you, your company, and your professional expertise.

Probing

1. Ask specific, factual questions.
2. Take detailed notes.
3. Ask "how" and "what" questions.
4. Encourage analyticals to discuss their feelings.
5. Be thorough, unhurried.
6. Summarize feedback the analytical has indicated is important. Be prepared to listen to additional details on these matters of importance.

Presenting

1. Provide a detailed written analysis of your solution.
2. The written proposal should be well-organized, logical, systematic, and practical.
3. Your proposal should stress how your solution will solve the analytical's problem.

Figure 3-3 Strategies for Dealing with the Analytical   (continues)

4. If you cannot answer a question specifically, offer to find the correct answer, and get back to the analytical with it.

5. Be reserved but not cold.

6. Avoid using emotional appeals.

7. Use specific examples. Recommend a specific course of action.

Closing

1. Ask for the order directly (in a low-key manner).

2. Use your standard order form or contract.

3. Expect to negotiate challenges and detail changes.

4. When answering objections, respond to the analytical's buying principles and objectivity.

Figure 3-3 Strategies for Dealing with the Analytical (continued)

into real fires, all the while seeming disappointed if others do not share their concerns about the importance of feeling as the necessary cornerstone for meaningful action and change.

Expressives are more oriented to the past than to other dimensions of time. It is the ability to draw on past experience and emotional interplay that makes expressives feel they can make the present meaningful to themselves or to others.

Among expressive types, one frequently finds entertainers, salesmen, writers, teachers, public relations specialists, nurses, social service workers, psychologists, psychiatrists, secretaries, retail businessmen, and realtors. Regardless of the job, individuals who extensively employ the expressive style are attracted by jobs or situations in which social-interpersonal contacts with others are highly likely.

Initial Contact. In establishing initial contact with expressives, you should forego written communication for a personal visit or a telephone call. You will find expressives to be the most responsive of all types to "cold" telephone or personal contact. Also, expressives will be most responsive to warmth, personalization, references to friends and acquaintances, and referral by someone they know. In regards to these references and referrals, the expressive will seek to know more about your relationship or connectedness with these people. If possible, refer to an acquaintance or friend who may use your product or service. Ideally, have that person set up the initial contact. Expressives may not be time-conscious and will often be late for meetings, so be prepared and do not schedule another appointment too close to your appointment with expressives. You need to make allowances for expressives' lateness and for their need to develop a relationship.

Expressives' secretaries may seem to have little difficulty connecting you with the prospects. Because expressives want to develop friendships, expressives are likely to grant you a meeting even if they are not especially interested in your product or service. In fact, expressives will be amenable to informal meetings—like lunch. You may be misled by this casual, friendly contact into expecting an easy sale; therefore, you are apt to prepare a low-key sales presentation when a harder line is really in order. The reality is that your time may be wasted on someone who has considerable curiosity and will look at all of the alternatives just to see what the market is like.

During the sales call, expressives will likely provide anecdotes and will expect you to do the same. Be prepared to tell stories about yourself. Keep in mind that expressives are least responsive to impersonal facts, figures, and details.

Recognizing the Expressive. The décor of expressives' offices are apt to be warm and colorful, and will be personalized with many mementos, photos of family and friends, meaningful knickknacks, and souvenirs. Citations for community or other social involvement may be displayed. Books of interest to expressives may include personal accounts and autobiographies, along with business-oriented materials. Expressives' dress may be casual, colorful, and perhaps flamboyant. Of all types, expressives are most apt to care how they appear—expressives may try to make an impression or a statement. Expressives may work for differing effects depending on mood and the people with whom they plan to be meet. Expressives are inclined to take time, if at all possible, learning about you and what you have to say. Expressives are also impulsive, and may make surprisingly rapid, incalculable decisions.

Sales Strategy for the Expressive. You should use your contacts with expressives. It is a good policy to relate how you were of service to someone the expressives know—expand the incident into a discussion of possible benefits to this sales situation. Hard facts may be in order, but expressives will be interested in who told you about them. Also, expressives will be inclined to use references you give to check results elsewhere, as this provides a legitimate reason to initiate contact with new people or old friends. Offer to put expressives in touch with satisfied customers with whom you have worked; expressives will respond to case histories of successful use. Expressives will be interested in anecdotes about product use and historical accounts of its progress.

You should attempt to link your product/service to people applications. That is, explain how you can help expressives solve problems for the people about whom they are concerned. Look for ways of establishing a climate of friendliness. Expressives may enjoy accepting a lunch or golf date to continue discussions. If you can, learn of their interests and relate to them; expressives appreciate the personalized approach.

During the presentation, make certain that you answer expressives' objections, and that you build a climate of warmth and trust. Try to demonstrate your efforts to cooperate and point out that you have expressives' best interests in mind, and that what you propose will be good for them as well as for the company. Solicit expressives' advice in helping you determine the best means of suiting your proposal to their needs, and ask for cooperation in setting up the final plan. Use an indirect or assumptive close to gain commitment from expressives. For a handy reference guide, see Strategies for Dealing with the Expressive in Figure 3-4.

Driver Type

Overview. The driver type places high value on action. "Drivers" thrive on getting things done here and now, without unnecessary and time-consuming deliberations. Drivers want to implement whatever they believe should be done and see the specific actions of others as better indicators of their

Positioning

1. Since letters are impersonal, the expressive may not take time to read them. Generally, a phone call is most appropriate. If you decide to write a letter, make it short, personal (telling who you are, who you know, why you're interested in the expressive).
2. Your phone call to the expressive should be open, friendly, stressing quick benefits, personal service, your experience, the experience of others.

Relating

1. Be on time (but don't always expect the expressive to be punctual).
2. Take time to develop the personal relationship based on openness and trust.
3. Feel free to engage in small talk.
4. Tell stories about people.
5. Talk about the expressive's personal interests.
6. Share your own feelings and enthusiasms.

Discovering

1. Probe for factual data you need for problem solving.
2. Use direct "who," "what," and "how" questions.
3. Listen responsively, giving plenty of nonverbal and verbal feedback to the expressive.
4. Show interest in and support of the expressive's goals.
5. Attempt to gain specifics from the expressive.
6. Summarize your findings, keeping the expressive's goals clearly in focus.

Advocating

1. Be specific and factual.
2. Don't overwhelm the expressive with details.
3. When possible, use third-party stories to support your proposal.
4. Offer incentives for quick action if possible.
5. Take time to develop ideas for implementation.
6. Try to get agreement/commitment to action in writing.
7. Don't rush the discussion, but try to keep it goal-directed.

Figure 3-4 Strategies for Dealing with the Expressive   (continues)

Supporting

1. Assume the sale.
2. Offer price break, value-added, or other incentives for immediate purchase when possible.
3. Answer objections with third-party stories or short case histories to show how others have overcome this same objection.
4. Get the order in writing.
5. Reaffirm your personal relationship with a personal follow-up.

Figure 3-4 Strategies for Dealing with the Expressive (continued)

commitments than any other response. Drivers engage in activities that provide opportunities for concrete, tangible, and immediate feedback. Drivers are likely, consequently, to express direct, down-to-earth, energetic approaches to work and life. Drivers never wish to "spin their wheels" worrying about the past, nor try to "crystal ball" the future. Drivers believe that if everyone else digs in their heels today, and gives the maximum effort toward meaningful goals, things will get done better and sooner.

Because the drivers' approaches are action-oriented and down to earth, they frequently are valued as driving forces within an organization. Drivers are seen as individuals who can be constructively relentless in the pursuit of measurable and high-quality results. Drivers are often sought out for their drive, and ability to translate ideas into products, sales, and profits.

Basically, drivers are doers, people who move ahead resourcefully and determinedly—overcoming sometimes seemingly insurmountable obstacles. Drivers thrive on working on a wide variety of projects and tasks at once, and yet often to others demonstrate what seems to be incredible attention to detail. Drivers feel comfortable committing to undertakings or even to other preliminary steps, however, only after they have been able to prove to themselves that the proposed action is likely to work. Drivers tend not to respect an idea until they have personally seen it translated into something practical and workable. If drivers cannot understand a proposed action in terms of their direct experience (who will do what; how; for what purpose; how will we know it is accomplished?), they may find it difficult or undesirable to proceed further with the matter. This reaction is because drivers tend to learn best, not on a conceptual or theoretical basis, but on the basis of immediate, direct, personal experience.

Drivers will usually be seen as decisive. Because drivers are impatient and non-indulgent of what they perceive as wasted time, they make rapid decisions. Quick decision-making is important to drivers because acting is one of their primary means of relieving anxiety or preventing wasted time from occurring. When there is indecision, drivers want to do something and are inclined to take action, even if only on a trial basis, to see if it works and, if so, how. Drivers tend to be impatient, and may frequently interrupt the conversation of others to get to the point. They dislike anecdotal material or minute detail that seems to cloud the issue or not get to the purpose of the discussion.

Drivers expect promptness, but may be late themselves because of their attempts to do more than they have time to accomplish. Drivers want you to state your case briefly, taking as little of time as is necessary to reach a decision. Loyalty is important to drivers, but drivers are likely to construe loyalty as a degree to which others agree with them and help them (even when they think the driver is wrong).

At their best, drivers are likely to be seen as dynamos—"herculean" workers who, once having committed to a task, will move mountains to make the undertaking a success. drivers are seen as growth-oriented, resourceful, well-organized, pragmatic, and hard-driving. Drivers usually impose high standards of utility on themselves and others. To this degree, drivers are likely to be seen as constructively impatient or tireless, doers par excellence. However, drivers may be seen as failing to consider sufficiently the long-range consequences of actions. That is, drivers may be seen as so action-oriented that they "short-circuit" significant steps in the planning process. In a sense, sometimes drivers dispense with caution and analysis in a cavalier fashion. Drivers can be criticized for imposing their expectations for drive, high speed, and zealousness onto others. At their worst, drivers tend to overemphasize short-term results and to act impulsively, trying to drive others to their will, rather than adopting strategies based on the concepts, plans, or feeling of others.

Among driver types, one frequently finds engineers, construction workers, bankers, market and financial analysts, military strategists, insurance managers, wholesalers, craftsmen, models, businessmen—particularly successful entrepreneurs as well as their secretaries—medical technicians, airline pilots, professional athletes, and physicians. Regardless of their job, individuals who extensively employ the driver style tend to be pragmatic and enjoy making things happen.

Initial Contact. Drivers, along with analyticals, may be difficult to contact "cold." However, you should still make the initial contact by telephone as an introductory letter may not be read. Drivers' secretaries may be trained to ask specific details and to be brief. The secretary may ask as a matter of form that you send a letter stating your interests, then follow up. If the prospects get on the phone, they may seem brusque or matter-of-fact. Drivers will expect to hear a plan resulting in an immediate benefit and will relate to how you have helped others in similar situations. Drivers will not be preoccupied with research in the matter, but rather with results. If interested, drivers will quickly arrive at a meeting time, and may tell you that they have little time to spare. Drivers do not respond to lengthy explanations or citations of data because of their impatience and sense of time pressure. If drivers say they are satisfied with a competitive supplier of the product/service you offer, try to buy time so that they do not end contact altogether. You should offer to send a letter with specific recommendations and take the initiative of a later follow-up. Drivers respond well to repeated contact as long as it does not weigh too seriously on their busy schedule. It may be best to approach drivers in "small doses."

Recognizing the Driver. Drivers will have a secretary show you into the office. Drivers may be conversing with someone, or on the phone when you appear. Drivers are inclined to be offhand, relatively abrupt, and matter-of-fact. Drivers want reports that are well organized, brief, and easy to scan for critical facts because they stay informed by quickly skimming material. Drivers' offices are most likely to have functional surroundings, and less likely to have collections of books and reports than the other social styles. However, it is more apt to be surrounded by clutter—several projects that they are in the midst of at once, and have too little time to get them all done. Drivers may be inclined toward decorations and photos that express action—mounted fishing or hunting trophies or racing prints.

In terms of dress, comfort is important to drivers. Therefore, drivers are inclined to simplicity, clothes that require little attention. If drivers bother, they may have an eye for color and quality.

Sales Strategies for the Driver. Results-oriented, drivers will be interested in where and how your proposal has worked for others, and how you can demonstrate that it will work for them. Drivers are susceptible to persuasion, have highly developed competitive sense, and will enjoy an effective sales pitch. Drivers want to hear brief, convincing points, and will be impressed with figures, but will not be especially interested in looking over quantities of data. Show drivers facts that can be grasped quickly and easily. Provide the bottom-line first, then work backward to the facts that support this final result.

Drivers will be impressed by dynamism, a no-nonsense approach, and a proposal that will make your point succinctly in a short amount of time. Keep in mind that drivers are not long on patience; be prepared to offer substantiating evidence after they have helped you make a fuller appraisal of needs. Interview drivers about what those needs might be; and offer to bring in whatever material the drivers require to corroborate your statements. Demonstrate that you have no intention of wasting their time, but are interested in giving the drivers exactly what they want so that they can make a decision on this matter. You should offer to return another time with information to buttress your contentions and to supply information drivers seek. Take the initiative in planning the next step. In all cases, make it simple for the drivers to alleviate any doubts they may have. Be prepared with positive suggestions for relieving pressures.

Drivers make decisions. If you are convincing in what you propose, and can offer evidence to substantiate it, drivers will likely decide in short order what they want to do. If you can show that you know your business, and offer drivers an easy way to work with you, drivers are more likely to decide in favor of your firm. Use a direct close with drivers. For an overview of this discussion, see Strategies for Dealing with the Driver in Figure 3-5.

Positioning

1. Drivers may not take time to read an introductory letter. You may prefer to make your first contact by phone, followed by a letter. The letter should confirm time and date of appointment and include any materials the driver may ask to review prior to the meeting.
2. The phone call to the driver should be businesslike and to the point. Take only enough time to identify yourself, explain your product/service and ask for an appointment.

Figure 3-5 Strategies for Dealing with the Driver   (continues)

Relating

1. Be on time. Drivers value punctuality and efficient use of their time.
2. Establish your competency with factual evidence of your professional expertise.
3. Use factual evidence to establish the soundness of your company and your product/service.
4. Be personable but reserved, relatively formal.
5. Focus your attention on the driver's ideas and objectives.
6. Listen carefully and provide factual answers to questions.

Discovering

1. Ask, don't tell.
2. Keep your questions factual, results oriented.
3. Use open-ended questions to allow the driver alternative ways of responding.
4. Phrase "feeling" questions in terms of results/consequences.
5. Listen carefully, selectively.
6. Support the driver's conclusions.
7. Summarize by feeding back your understanding of the driver's priorities.

Advocating

1. Offer options and probabilities.
2. Be specific and factual without overwhelming with details.
3. Compare alternative solutions and their probable outcomes.
4. Let the driver choose his or her course of action.
5. Be accurate, clear, concise.

Supporting

1. Ask for the order directly.
2. Offer options.
3. Have an alternative proposal ready.
4. Be prepared to negotiate, modify your proposal.
5. Think through possible objections in advance and be prepared to answer them with facts.
6. Answer objections in ways that respond to the driver's ideas, objectives, and conclusions.

Figure 3-5 Strategies for Dealing with the Driver (continued)

If you fail to adapt your social style to that of your customer, you may be perceived in a less than flattering light. This section discusses interactions between the various social styles and how each social style perceives the other *if the appropriate adaptation does not take place.*

If your social style is AMIABLE, the *ANALYTICAL* is likely to regard your approach as too broad-brush, abstract, "far-out," untested, a radical departure from the past, flaunting tradition, blue-sky, and insufficiently documented. Similarly, you may "turn off" the *EXPRESSIVE* who is likely to regard your approach as intellectualized, theoretical, unintelligible, "okay from a book standpoint, not for our people," too complex, lacking in structure, unspecific as to people terms, threatening, and something "we're not ready for." Finally, you may distance the *DRIVER* who is likely to regard your sales approach as "pie in the sky," idealistic, puffery, free-form, not useful (even if it happens to be right), an egotistical trip, and typical of ivory-tower thinking.

If your social style is ANALYTICAL, the *AMIABLE* is likely to regard your typical approach as pedantic, cautious, lacking vision, belabored, repetitious, overly responsive to immediate constraints, unimaginative, a slight refinement "when what we really need is a new way of thinking," conservative, and overly locked into tradition and past practice. You may also annoy the *EXPRESSIVE* who is likely to regard your approach as mechanistic, cut and dried, lacking enthusiasm, playing it safe, numerical, over-structured, lacking spontaneity, too formal, lacking a light touch, tradition-bound, fearful, defensive, overly test-oriented, and more concerned with form and your own image than in bringing about a real breakthrough. Lastly, you may offend the *DRIVER* who is likely to regard your approach as unnecessarily complicated; too research-oriented and insufficiently action-oriented; overly analytical—insufficiently geared to the bottom line; hedging and avoiding a specific commitment to when, what, how much, etc.; too locked into "if this, then that . . . ;" lacking "guts;" and too much by the book.

If your social style is EXPRESSIVE, the *AMIABLE* is likely to regard your approach as worrisome, overactive, lacking in vision, too concerned with the feelings of "others who demonstrate faulty judgment themselves," superficial; lacking conceptual underpinnings, too concerned with politics, emphasizing "stop-gap" or "pro temp" solutions, relying on gimmicks, and opportunistic. The *ANALYTICAL* is likely to regard your sales approach as impulsive; slapdash; insufficiently thought through, not researched; relying on "gut feel," not facts; lacking documentation; untested, proceeding on faith; having failed to weigh or delineate options; having committed without sufficient thought to resources; failing to forecast outcomes; naive; too easily swayed by others; premature; and not following established and sound methods. Finally, the *DRIVER* is likely to perceive your approach as innovative but impractical; more concerned with people's sensitivities than "hard, bottom-line" results; free-form; inconsistent and different from positions you've advocated before; perceptive but "blue-sky . . . not battened down" in terms of next steps, specific assignments, timetables or expected results; immature; blowing things out of proportion; thin-skinned; defensive; more concerned with possibilities than action; and better in your start-up ideas than in your finishing, windup strategies.

If your social style is DRIVER, you may alienate the *AMIABLE* who is likely to perceive your approach as simplistic; too concerned with the immediate crisis of this week, this month, this quarter; overly preoccupied with short-term results at the expense of long-term direction, policy, fundamentals; the proverbial "bull-in-a-china-shop;" ego-centered; too swayed by outside competitive pressures; "shooting from the hip;" opportunistic; too commercially oriented; insufficiently professional; "putting the cart before the horse;" and not mindful of long-term objectives. The *ANALYTICAL* may regard your approach as piecemeal; shrewd, but lacking depth; committing prematurely; changeable; impulsive; lacking a systematic approach; not utilizing a team approach; insufficiently building on progress of past; shortsighted; not allowing enough time, money or resources for research and development; vague as to objectives and specific program phases; crisis-oriented; "so concerned with cash flow that you'll escalate costs unreasonably to get sales volume;" lacking an orderly, sound, tested business approach; and simply "lucky." The *EXPRESSIVE* is likely to perceive your approach as insensitive; task-oriented; ramrodding others; premature; stubborn; pushing people rather than influencing them; authoritarian; more concerned with ends than means or processes; insufficiently listening; walking over people; suspicious; old guard; too risk-oriented; not mindful of past loyalties and relationships.

The preceding discussion should demonstrate to you the importance of adapting to the social styles of your customers. For an overview, see Table 3-2, Dealing with Each Personality Style in the Presentation.

If by chance you find yourself selling to someone you have identified as possessing your own social style, you will not have to make the same adjustments as you would if the customer were of a different social style. For example, the customer with an identical social style will likely see you as intelligent, perceptive, and "on his/her wavelength." Because this customer is likely to reinforce your own social style, you may say too much, over-control, and tend to dominate. Consequently, you must be careful to (1) listen; (2) draw the customer out; and (3) not overplay your advantage. Also, although the customer may commit quickly to your plan or strategy because your thinking is similar, this is not always a good thing. If possible, you should solicit independent feedback from someone whose style is the opposite of yours and build this input into your strategic approach.

Social Styles Exercises

Exercise 1

You find yourself working for Raymark Conference Center. As part of your new sales position, you have managed to wrangle an appointment with Janet Smith, vice president of sales for ACME Service Corporation. Normally, your sales manager would accompany you on such an important sales call, but he has been unexpectedly called away due to a family matter. As it took some time to land the appointment, you don't dare cancel. When you arrive at the ACME Service Corporation, you are directed to Ms. Smith's office. A secretary greets you and tells you that Ms. Smith will be with you shortly. You have a seat in the reception area and note that you are 10 minutes early for your appointment; you use the time to look over your presentation notes one last time. At the appointed hour, you hear the secretary's buzzer. You are told that Ms. Smith will now see you, and you are escorted into her office.

You approach Ms. Smith and introduce yourself; she's not terribly cold, but not overly friendly either. You note that Ms. Smith is dressed very nicely, but formally, in a dark conservative business

Table 3-2: Dealing with Each Personality Style In the Presentation

Analyticals

Use a direct approach
Stick to specifics
Don't overstate
List advantages and disadvantages
Put things in writing
Provide evidence
Don't rush, but be persistent
Emphasize technical details

Drivers

Maintain a business-like relationship
Don't waste time—be clear, specific, and brief
Be precise
Demonstrate "bottom-line" performance
Show increase in driver's control
Be organized in your presentation

Amiables

Develop a personal relationship first
Provide personal assurances and guarantees
Emphasize how your product affects people
Discuss personal opinions
Don't rush; present your case softly
Show interest in them as people

Expressives

Be entertaining, stimulating, fun loving
Use testimonials
Appeal to status and recognition needs
Talk about people
Develop a personal relationship

suit with a white shirt and dark pumps. Although the office is quite large with a great view of the city, the furnishings are primarily functional, not opulent. You notice sales graphs and charts on her desk as well as a large stack of what appears to be sales data. You catch a glimpse of her computer screen and note it displays an Excel spreadsheet. Ms. Smith tells the secretary that she will see her next appointment in 20 minutes—you now know that you don't have much time to make your point.

You explain that, as a representative of Raymark, you are interested in serving the needs of the ACME Service Corporation, and that you would like to better understand those needs. You tell Ms.

Smith that Raymark has a truly luxurious, yet functional conference center that focuses on accommodating the special needs of corporate groups. Ms. Smith wants to know exactly how you do that. In response, you take out five or six letters of testimony from several corporations. She studies them in great detail.

a. What primary social style does Ms. Smith possess? What has led you to that conclusion?

_____

_____

_____

b. Based on Ms. Smith's social style, how should you structure your sales presentation? What do you want to do? What do you want to avoid doing? Be specific.

_____

_____

_____

c. What is your social style? How would your own social style be perceived by Ms. Smith? In other words, how would your social style interact with her social style?

_____

_____

_____

Exercise 2

You are employed by USA Airlines. As part of your new sales position, you have obtained an appointment with Martin Larsen, vice president of logistics and distribution for a large retail chain called Sky Limited. When you arrive at Sky Limited's headquarters, you are directed to Mr. Larsen's office. A secretary greets you and tells you that Mr. Larsen will be with you shortly. You have a seat in the reception area and since you are early for your appointment, you use the time to look over your presentation notes one last time. Ten minutes after the appointed hour, you hear the secretary's buzzer. You are told that Mr. Larsen will now see you, and you are escorted into his office. Mr. Larsen meets you at the door and gives you a hearty handshake. Mr. Larsen tells the secretary that he will see his next appointment in 20 minutes—you now know that you don't have much time to make your point.

You note that Mr. Larsen is dressed nicely, but comfortably; he has a slightly rumpled look. Although the office is large with a great view of the city, every piece of furniture appears to have stacks of paper on it. Mr. Larsen hurriedly removes some papers from a chair so that you can have a seat. The phone rings and you hear Mr. Larsen tell the other party to "just get it done." While he's on the phone, you notice a few framed action shots of what appears to be Mr. Larsen skydiving and bungee jumping.

You explain that, as a representative of USA Airlines, you are interested in serving the needs of Sky Limited, and that you would like to better understand what those needs are. Mr. Larsen tells you he doesn't have time to explain everything about Sky Limited—"Exactly what is it you want to know?" You begin to talk about the services that USA Airlines could offer Sky Limited, but Mr. Larsen interrupts to ask, "Just how much will the shipments cost?"

a. What primary social style does Mr. Larsen possess? What has led you to that conclusion?

_____

_____

_____

b. Based on Mr. Larsen's social style, how should you structure your sales presentation? What do you want to do? What do you want to avoid doing? Be specific.

_____

_____

_____

c. What is your social style? How would your own social style be perceived by Mr. Larsen, if you fail to adapt? In other words, how would your social style interact with his social style?

_____

_____

_____

  ## Customer Mapping and Social Styles Exercise

Return to your customer map in the Preapproach section, and for each buyer you have named, identify the buyer's social style. This information will assist you in conversing with and preparing a presentation for each buyer. Further, identifying the social styles of your buyers will help you later determine the benefits and personal "wins" each one is seeking.

Once You've "Read" the Customer, Remember to Apply Your Sales Strategy Model!

1. Pre-Read Client.

Diagnose the customer's probable primary social style.

2. **Anticipate Style Conflict.**

   Use self-diagnostic data to determine probable conflict between the customer's social style and yours.

3. **Map Your Sales Content Strategy.**

   Collect, organize, and dry run all relevant facts and benefits to the customer and customer's company.

4. **Map Your Consultative Style Strategy.**

   Determine the social style you will use to effectively interact with the customer. Check for self-consistency in correspondence, phone contact, sales materials, etc.

5. **Validate and Modify.**

   In face-to-face contacts with customer, validate or reject the preliminary diagnosis of his or her social style data and modify your consultative social style accordingly.

6. **Use Conflict Management Techniques.**

   Use silence, acceptance, open questions, directive questions, restatement, and reflection to create social style harmony.

7. **Use Appropriate Style Close.**

   Employ a final closing strategy tailored to the customer's social style.

8. **Reinforce Strategically.**

   After the sale is completed, gear your follow-up actions to key customers and "secondary customers" within the client company. Remember: good service on past sales is the key to future sales opportunities.

Key Concepts

Chapter 3 initiates an exploration of the approach stage of the sales process. The primary points of this chapter are:

- Adaptive selling, the ability to use different sales approaches in different situations, is a key factor in sales success.
- Adaptive selling is facilitated by knowledge of customer categories, as defined by the social style grid. Social style grid categories consist of amiable, analytical, expressive, and driver.
- Amiables are imaginative, people-oriented, and future-oriented. They seek to form friendship bonds with selected salespeople as a reassurance the amiables will receive fair treatment in the sales process/transaction. Amiables require a soft-sell approach, guarantees, and third-party references.

- Analyticals are fact-oriented, extremely organized, and weigh decisions carefully. They do not want relationships with salespeople and they dislike sales "puffery." Analyticals require a formal approach. Written and verbal proposals to analyticals should provide event steps or phases to emphasize organization. All statements by the salesperson should be supported by evidence.

- Expressives are people-oriented and outgoing. They value relationships above all else and will want to form relationships with salespeople. Expressives enjoy talking, so salespeople should allow for extra time when calling on expressives. After establishing a good relationship with expressives, the salesperson should assume the sale in closing.

- Drivers are fact- and action-oriented. They do not seek relationships with salespeople, but are willing to make rapid buying decisions, even with only partial information. The salesperson should focus on the "bottom-line" benefits to the driver and utilize a direct close.

Endnotes

[1] Spiro, Rosann L. and Barton A. Weitz (1990), "Adaptive Selling: Conceptualization, Measurement and Nomological Validity," *Journal of Marketing Research* 27 (February), 61-9.

[2] Merrill, David and Roger Reid (1981), *Personal Styles and Effective Performance: Make Your Style Work for You.* Radnor, PA: Chilton.

Approach through Nonverbal Communication, Listening, and Trust

his chapter continues to examine the approach stage of the sales process. Specifically, it describes the importance of using appropriate body language to get the sales message across, as well as how to read and adapt to the nonverbal expressions of the buyer. Next explained are the importance of being a good listener, including specific tips on how to improve listening habits and how to develop active listening skills. Finally, material is presented concerning the importance of facilitating a trusting relationship and identifying the factors deemed necessary in developing and maintaining trust. The chapter concludes by describing how quickly trust can be lost when a customer becomes angry or upset, and what steps the salesperson can undertake to avoid a complete loss of trust.

Clues to Body Language

People use **body language** to communicate. Indeed body language may more accurately convey emotions than the spoken word, therefore, it is important to be able to read the prospective buyer's nonverbal communication. Understanding nonverbal communication requires interpretation of body angle, facial expression, arm movement or position, hand movements or position, and leg position. Used in combination with one another, these various communication modes can send favorable, neutral, or unfavorable signals, which you must interpret correctly in order to respond in an appropriate manner.[1]

Favorable Body Language. Favorable body language signals that the prospect is interested in what you are saying and is willing to listen. Favorable communication modes include:

Body angle	Upright or leaning slightly forward.
Face	Smiling, accepting expression; relaxed jaw, good eye contact or eyes scanning visual aids, pleasant voice.
Hands	Open and relaxed; perhaps taking notes or performing calculations; holding a product sample or visual aid; firm, friendly handshake.
Arms	Relaxed and open; not crossed.
Legs	Crossed and pointed toward you or uncrossed, feet flat on the floor.

Neutral Body Language. Neutral body language may indicate disbelief, disinterest, or withdrawal; consequently, the prospect is not open to what you are saying. Neutral signals are dangerous because they may quickly become unfavorable signals if you do not take action to turn the situation around.

Body angle	Leaning back or away from you.
Face	Confused or bored expression; poor or irregular eye contact; puzzled or neutral voice tone; hardly any verbal comments or asking few, if any, questions; head moving side to side.
Arms	Crossed.
Hands	Fidgeting hands; weak handshake; no attempt to hold product or visual aids; scratching head; pulling at ear; hands clasped together.
Legs	Crossed away from you.

Unfavorable Body Language. Unfavorable signals indicate hostility or anger and a complete breakdown of communication. You should *immediately* alter the course of your presentation and resort to procedures for handling angry customers.

Body angle	Positioned to move away from you; leaning as far away as possible from you.
Face	Tightened jaw line; visibly displaying anger through furrowed brow and clenched mouth; slow shaking of head to indicate disagreement; little eye contact or angrily staring; unpleasant voice tones or suddenly silent; frequently glances at watch.
Arms	Crossed over chest; rigid.
Hands	Waving you away; making a fist; hands rigidly flat on table; tense, weak handshake.
Legs	Crossed and turned away from you, as to exit room.

Be careful not to mimic the body language of an angry prospect or customer, and refrain from adopting gestures or movements indicating defensiveness or an urge to withdraw from the situation. Retain an open, nonconfrontational position with feet flat on the floor, hands and arms open, and body angled slightly forward. Maintain good eye contact, a positive attitude, and a pleasant facial expression. In other words, practice favorable body language.

Listening Skills

Good **listening skills** have long been recognized as essential to success.[2] In fact, Socrates once complained that the youths he tutored were generally appalling listeners. Most people spend about half of their waking hours listening, yet research studies show that they retain about 20 to 25 percent of what is heard, a very low efficiency level.[3] This finding is not surprising since listening is the one communication skill no one is ever really taught, and thus, most complacent about. We are taught how to read, to write, to speak, but not to listen. We think that if our ears are normal we can hear everything that goes on around us. This line of thinking is good as far as hearing goes, but listening and hearing are not the same.

- Hearing means registering the sound vibrations.
- Listening means making sense out of what is heard.

There's a lot more to listening than hearing. After we hear something, we must interpret it, evaluate it, and finally respond to it—that's listening. And it is during this complex process that people run into all kinds of trouble. For example:

- People prejudge—sometimes even disregard—a speaker based on that person's delivery or appearance.
- People let personal ideas, emotions or prejudices distort what a speaker has to say.
- People tune out subjects considered too difficult or uninteresting. Because the brain works four times faster than most people speak, we too often wander into distraction.

During a sales call on a customer, you should be listening, rather than talking, 50 to 80 percent of the time.[4] Take the listening skills quiz shown in Figure 4-1, Measuring Your Listening Skills. Note the areas where your listening skills are likely to be weak (i.e., 1 or 2), and seek to identify ways in which you can improve. Your total score should be 30 or above. If it is less than 30, then you need to enhance your overall listening ability.

Obstacles to Effective Listening
There are a number of obstacles that can interfere with listening. Take the necessary steps to overcome each of the problems causing an obstacle to improve how effectively you listen to your customers and prospects.

Environmental Interference
Conduct your meeting in an atmosphere that is as conducive as possible to effective communication between you and your buyer. That is, try to avoid making your presentation in an environment that is noisy or otherwise distracting to you and/or your buyer.

Divided Attention (Speaker or Listener)
Make sure that your transition from speaker to listener is a complete one. Don't be thinking about what you will say next while the buyer is talking.

Read the questions below and rate each of your listening characteristics using the following system:

Always . . . . 4 points
Almost always . . . . 3 points
Rarely . . . . 2 points
Never . . . . 1 point

Listening Characteristics

1. I allow the speaker to express his or her complete thoughts without interrupting
| 4 | 3 | 2 | 1 |

2. I listen between the lines, especially when conversing with individuals who frequently use hidden meanings
| 4 | 3 | 2 | 1 |

3. I actively try to develop retention ability so I can remember important facts
| 4 | 3 | 2 | 1 |

4. I write down the most important details of a message
| 4 | 3 | 2 | 1 |

5. In recording a message, I concentrate on writing the major facts and the key phrases
| 4 | 3 | 2 | 1 |

6. I read back essential details to the speaker before the conversation ends to ensure correct understanding
| 4 | 3 | 2 | 1 |

7. I refrain from turning off the speaker because the message is dull or boring, or because I do not personally know or like the speaker
| 4 | 3 | 2 | 1 |

8. I avoid becoming hostile or excited when a speaker's views differ from my own
| 4 | 3 | 2 | 1 |

9. I ignore distractions when listening
| 4 | 3 | 2 | 1 |

10. I express a genuine interest in the other individual's conversation
| 4 | 3 | 2 | 1 |

Total:

Figure 4-1 Measuring Your Listening Skills

Fear of Failure.

The fear that your sales proposition will end negatively is a great obstacle to overcome, which sometimes causes the salesperson to talk incessantly. Try to relax and proceed conversationally; know when to stop talking.

Indifference.

Sometimes individuals feel that what a customer is telling them is not important, so they tune that person out, allowing their minds to wander. Customers will convey their needs if you listen closely.

Impatience.

Salespeople may become impatient with a slow or rambling speaker and their thoughts begin to race ahead of the conversation. You may miss some crucial clue that could help you close the sale.

Prejudice.

Sometimes salespeople allow prejudice to arise—such as the way the customer speaks, the customer's attitudes or those of the customer's company—and so must learn to control those prejudices. It is important that you remain vigilant during sales calls so this does not interfere with your goal.

Misuse of Words.

Sometimes the seller or buyer is guilty of misuse of words and one or both persons may be confused or misinterpret the message. It is important to ask questions if you suspect that the customer is not clear or shows signs of confusion.

How to Improve Listening Habits

Below are some tips you can use to improve your listening habits. See if you can incorporate them into your everyday routine.

Don't Interrupt.

Interruptions stifle communications. When a salesperson interrupts a customer's train of thought, his or her own listening is also interrupted. Constant interruption will result in a customer's reluctance to talk and will most certainly become irritated with the salesperson.

Listen for Between-the-Lines Messages.

It is only through intent listening that someone can determine the real meaning of what is said. Listen between the lines by being observant of both the customer's nonverbal communication and what you see around you.

Concentrate on Developing Retention Skills.

Try to retain all information by good retention skills rather than by writing everything down. Sometimes, however, you may need to take notes and in that case it is a useful tool. It tells the customer that you are serious and concerned.

Don't Tune Out The Speaker.

If the customer is a rambler, or even a bore for that matter, do not tune that person out. First, you would be developing lazy listening habits that can interfere with valuable input and second, you may be missing a valuable piece of information. Try to gently return the customer to the subject at hand.

Don't Become Emotional or Hostile.
When you disagree with the customer's point of view, never become angry. There will be ample time to present your point of view during your presentation. If you disagree with something unrelated to business, your feelings are best left unsaid.

Learn to Ignore Distractions.
It is useful to remember that while business activity in the customer's office might distract you, it is likely that the customer is acclimated to such activity and may not be affected as you are.

Active Listening
Active listening is the ability to rephrase client conversation in order to gain concurrence, check for understanding, and keep the discussion moving. Active listening involves rephrasing, summarizing, and paraphrasing to check for understanding. Consequently, practicing active listening provides a number of benefits to both you and your customer: (1) the customer will give you facts, (2) you will verify your understanding of the facts, and (3) through rephrasing you will clarify information and allow for summarization.

Examples of lead-in phrases are:

- "If I understand you correctly . . . "
- "Let me see if I have this . . . "
- "So what I hear you saying is . . . "

The key to rephrasing is to choose your own words, and to make a statement (or question) that summarizes the client's thoughts. When rephrasing customer information, you give the customer a chance to change or correct the information ("No, that's not it/Yes, but . . . "), to elaborate ("Yes, and . . . "), or to agree ("Yes, that's it").

Examples:

Client:	"I have an experienced sales force but we have not seen any significant increase in sales. They have too long of a sales cycle requiring too many meetings with clients."
Salesperson:	(Rephrasing) "So you are saying that the salespeople are taking too long to close sales?"
Client:	(Corrects) "Taking too long to close the sale is a problem for some, but they all lack a systematic approach to customer meetings."
Salesperson:	(Rephrasing) "In other words, you believe the sales organization needs to focus on an organized procedure?"

Client:	(Elaborates) "Yes, with the changes in technology, I see new opportunity. I believe they need a refresher meeting."
Salesperson:	(Summarizes) "As I understand it then, you would like us to provide meeting space for a refresher sales course in the near future?"
Client:	(Agrees) "That's right."

Several outcomes will result from your effort at rephrasing and summarizing customer comments. The relationship will be enhanced because the customer will recognize that you are paying close attention to what is said. As a result, the customer will feel that he or she has value and importance, and you will be seen as professional and caring. Thus, the customer will be willing to share more information and the conversation will advance.

Developing and Maintaining Trust

Trust is crucial to almost every business relationship, especially in one where the product or service is largely intangible, as in the hospitality industry. Unfortunately, trust is not immediately present on an initial sales call. Indeed, real trust is built over time—not in a single call or over a short period of time. Trust is only developed after a number of interactions have occurred. And while trust is difficult to develop, it is easy to lose!

There are some steps, however, that you can use to foster perceptions of trust even in the first sales visit. These perceptions depend upon your knowledge, as well as your firm. Basically, there are five factors you can display to build the customer's trust in you:[5]

Customer Orientation. The buyer's needs are placed at the forefront of your concerns. You give balanced presentations (pros and cons) and clearly identify the benefits of your product or service.

Expertise. You are knowledgeable and accurate about your product and those of your competitors. You project a professional image. You have the skills and resources to meet customer needs.

Reliability. You do what you promise and do not promise what you cannot deliver.

Candor. You are honest and you provide proof to support your words. You respond truthfully even when it hurts. You do not reveal confidential information, and you speak well of other customers and competitors.

Likeability. You are considerate of the buyer's time and courteous to all around you. You adapt to the buyer's social style and establish communication on topics (including nonbusiness) that are of interest to the buyer. You smile often, and maintain a positive, enthusiastic attitude.

How can you convey these five factors to your customers? Think of a prospect you have recently identified. Then using the chart in Figure 4-2, below each factor, list at least three means by which you would demonstrate these traits to your prospective buyer.

Customer Orientation   Expertise   Reliability

_____   _____   _____

_____   _____   _____

_____   _____   _____

            Candor   Likeability

        _____   _____

        _____   _____

        _____   _____

Figure 4-2 Factors for Developing Trust

Managing Angry Customers

Sometimes despite your best efforts, a customer may become angry with you. In these cases, the customer may have a legitimate reason for being angry. Perhaps you failed to follow up, or you did not convey the customer's explicit directions to the right members of the service staff. At other times, the problem may actually be a result of the customer's failure to do or say something. Whatever the cause, it is up to you to take steps to re-establish a trusting relationship. Failure to respond immediately can mean the loss of not only this customer's future business, but the business of all the acquaintances of this customer who may receive negative word-of-mouth communications.

There are four key rules for managing people who are angry and upset:

1. _Don't try to control or threaten people who are angry._ You can't control another person's anger; but you can show understanding. A good way to do this is just to allow them to be angry without criticizing or somehow trying to get them to stop expressing their anger. Give them some time to share their anger and talk about it.

2. _Show you care. Empathize. Show understanding about how your client feels._ For example, you can say something like, "I understand how you feel, and I see that getting what you ordered is a major concern at this time. I'd be angry, too, if that happened to me." It's probably best to stay with allowing the customer to express his anger but do not be tempted to say something like: "You're right, our kitchen staff can't ever seem to get special orders done correctly. It's infuriating, I know." In-house criticism is not going to be very helpful to the people involved.

3. *A third key rule for handling angry customers is to assure the client that the anger will not jeopardize the relationship.* For example, you can say, "I understand your reaction and appreciate your openness. You see this gives me a chance to work harder for you." Or you can say something like, "I'm sure you realize your business is very important to me." Then after your clients have had time to vent their anger, you can clarify, diagnose, and respond to the real issues. "Now, could you help me understand the details of this problem?" Once you have allowed the venting of angry feelings, you can begin to think through what the problem is and see if some new answers can be established. This period is a time when you can renegotiate and build new bridges in the relationship. This rebuilding is very difficult to do if the person has not had a chance to get his angry feelings put forward. Any attempts on your part to block those feelings because of fear or anxiety will get in the way of your continuing the relationship and bridging on to new business.

4. *Watch out for your nonverbal expressions.* It is a good idea not to mirror the client's negative, nonverbal expressions. Don't withdraw, don't show defensiveness; work to express an open posture. Look at the person without challenge, but with caring. Crossing your legs and arms will only show a desire to retreat on your part and make it more difficult to establish communication with your customer.

When you encounter a customer who is obviously upset and angry, but is also silent, you have a big problem. You can tell the person is annoyed by a clenched jaw, averted glance, and unwillingness to communicate openly or directly. The problem is difficult for you because you do not have any information. You do not know what the problem is and it seems embarrassing or too personal to ask. The customer has a key advantage. The customer is in the passive manipulating position and can create feelings in you of self-doubt and insecurity. You stand around wondering what you did wrong. To counter the silent, angry customer, you can ask questions that are essentially statements about the customer's silence:

- "Is there anything about me or my company that prevents you from doing business with us?"
- "I can't help noticing that I have been doing most of the talking, and at this point I'd like to ask you what seems to hold you back from expressing your objective opinion."
- "Obviously, you must have a reason for saving your opinion on what we've been discussing. Would you mind if I asked what it is?"

If you use these techniques, be prepared to accept open anger. You may push a button that will help the person express anger and hostility directly. Then you can revert to the strategies mentioned above of listening and allowing the person to vent his or her anger, and then sit down with the person to discuss and renegotiate your situation. While you may believe that a silently angry customer is easier to handle than an openly angry customer, just the opposite is true. An openly angry customer at least provides you with the information needed to resolve the problem.

Steps for Handling Angry or Upset Customers. Here are specific steps you should use to respond to an angry or upset customer:

1. Encourage angry customers to tell their story. Ask the right questions to get silent, but angry customers talking.

2. Express regret for any inconvenience.

3. Reassure the customer that the company wants to be fair.

4. Discuss points of agreement and get the facts. If possible, examine the product in front of the customer.

5. Gain agreement on responsibility for the problem.

6. Gain agreement on a solution.

7. Take action immediately.

8. Educate and resell the customer to prevent additional complaints.

9. Follow through on promised action.

Angry Customer Role-Play Exercise

Use this role-play exercise to practice incorporating the nine steps for handling angry or upset customers. Ask a friend or colleague to play the role of the angry buyer. Have the friend role-play as though openly angry the first time, then repeat the exercise with the friend playing the part of a silently angry customer. Analyze which type of angry customer is easier to handle. The following includes background information that both participants should read:

Lee Martin is the general manager of Limited Investments, a local investment firm. Lee has held this position for about one and a half years. Limited Investments holds monthly investment seminars for prospective clients, during which a continental breakfast is served. Your hotel (Sheldon House) has been the site for these monthly seminars for years. This last year for some reason, the hotel has not been receiving payments regularly. The last payment, $355.75, is now a month overdue. And for months before that, payments ranged anywhere from one to three months behind. However, in all these cases, the hotel has eventually received its money.

Your staff has traditionally complained about the Limited manager always giving the staff a "hard time." He frequently changes the number of expected attendees at the last minute, and expects the staff to alter the room setup and amount of food ordered accordingly. When fewer guests arrive than guaranteed, he expects to pay only for the actual number of guests at the breakfast. This puts pressure on the staff and results in wasted food. He gripes regularly to your staff about the room not being set up properly, the coffee not being hot enough, or the muffins not being fresh enough, and just generally expects a lot of favors even though this is one of the hotel's smallest accounts. There has been a high turnover of wait staff, and this probably will continue because of the low pay your company can afford to give them. You know the staff has not been giving good service lately, but much of the problem simply is their anger at this manager, Lee Martin.

This particular account, because of its size, is not very important to your overall hotel profits. You would like to maintain them as an account simply because you feel accounts of this nature add up to significant volume. However, you are not very interested in having to make a lot of concessions on your part to get the matter resolved (i.e., the late payments). Your objective of this meeting is to collect the payment and to reiterate the company policies (i.e., confirming the party size at least seven days in advance, that you cannot give credit for unused food because a party is smaller than anticipated).

1. Conduct the role-play exercise. The seller should attempt to achieve his or her objective.

2. If no resolution has occurred in 10 minutes, stop the exercise. The buyer should complete the following evaluation form for the salesperson.

3. The "buyer" should answer the following questions and provide feedback to the salesperson. Did the salesperson try to control or threaten you?

Did the salesperson show that he or she cared about your needs and concerns?

Did the salesperson assure you that your anger will not jeopardize the relationship?

Did the salesperson manage his or her feelings of anger and nonverbal expressions effectively?

Key Concepts

Chapter 4 completes the approach phase of the sales process by examining the importance of body language, listening, and developing trust. Specifically, this chapter has discussed these concepts:

- Body language often conveys far more than the spoken word; thus, the salesperson must practice utilizing positive, open body language: leaning slightly forward; smiling; good eye contact; open, relaxed hands and arms; legs uncrossed, feet flat on floor. The salesperson must also be prepared to understand what message is being revealed by the body language of the buyer.

- Listening requires paying attention and accurately interpreting what is said. The salesperson should be listening during 50 to 80 percent of the sales presentation.

- Active listening techniques should be employed by the salesperson to gain concurrence, to check for understanding, and to keep the discussion moving forward.

- Trust is a crucial element in any business relationship. Five factors foster perceptions of trust in the salesperson: customer orientation, expertise, reliability, candor, and likeability. Trust can be difficult to gain, but can be lost very quickly.

- When trust has been lost, the salesperson should seek to re-establish a trusting relationship by following the nine steps for managing an angry customer.

Endnotes

[1] The body language described herein was adapted from Futrell, Charles (1997), *ABC's of Relationship Selling*, 5th ed., Chicago: Irwin; and Gschwandtner, Gerhard (1982) "Closing Sales via Body Signals," *Marketing Times* 29 (September/October),12-13.

[2] Castleberry, Stephen B., C. David Shepherd, and Rick Ridnour (1999), "Effective Interpersonal Listening in the Personal Selling Environment: Conceptualization, Measurement, and Nomological Validity," *Journal of Marketing Theory and Practice* 7 (Winter), 30-38; Boorom, Michael L., Jerry R. Goolsby, and Rosemary P. Ramsey (1998), "Relational Communication Traits and Their Effect on Adaptiveness and Sales Performance," *Journal of the Academy of Marketing Science* 26 (Winter), 16-30.

[3] Metcalf, Tom (1997), "Listening to Your Clients," *Life Association News* 92 (July), 16-17.

[4] Brooks, Bill (2000) "Listening Versus Talking: The Revolving Ratio," *The American Salesman* 45 (July), 20-23.

[5] Adapted from Hawes, Jon M., Kenneth E. Mast and John E. Swan (1989), "Trust Earning Perceptions of Sellers and Buyers," *The Journal of Personal Selling & Sales Management* 9 (Spring), 1-8.

5

OPENINGS

ood openings are important to the sales process. After all, you only have one chance to make a good first impression. Consequently, the first 30 seconds could be the most important time you will spend with the buyer in any visit. Strong openings are designed to accomplish four goals: (1) gain the attention of the prospect, (2) break into the prospect's stream of thought, (3) arouse the prospect's interest in your proposal, and (4) allow you to secure control of the interaction. To achieve these goals, your opening should use the information you previously gathered in the preapproach stage, tie into your objective for the sales call, be well planned, and finally, be tailored specifically for the prospect. This latter component means you should develop the opening around the prospect's discovered needs and social style.

Opening Techniques

Your effectiveness during the opening moments determines how receptive the buyer will be, how difficult or easy the close will be, and how welcome you will be on the follow-up visits. Remember, to be effective, the opening must accomplish three things in the following order: (1) Break into the buyer's train of thought and neutralize what was in the buyer's mind, (2) establish in the buyer's mind what you wish to sell, and (3) arouse his or her interest in your proposition.

The best attention getter is a specific owner benefit that appeals to a specific need or want of the buyer. Owner benefits that affect the prospect's self, hopes, wishes, desires, and circumstances are very powerful attention getters. A second method for getting the prospect's attention is to mention some matter of universal interest, such as ecology, purchasing power of the prospect's customers, technology, other current news, happenings or matters of common concern.

You should recognize that there are many types of openings that are available to you. Although only a limited number will be identified here, you should become comfortable with many different types of openings and tailor the opening you use based on the individual prospect with whom you will be interacting.

Openings by Telephone

The telephone is routinely used in hospitality sales and most frequently will be the first mode of contact with a prospective client. Guidelines[1] for proper handling regarding incoming phone calls include the following list:

1. Answer the telephone promptly, preferably by the third ring.

2. Keep information sheets organized and close at hand so you do not waste the caller's time while you search for needed data.

3. Identify yourself and your department. For example, "Good afternoon. Sales department. This is Mary. How may I help you?"

4. Do not chew gum, smoke, eat, or drink while speaking over the telephone.

5. Obtain the name of caller, caller's company, address, and telephone number at the beginning of the call.

6. Use the client's name often. Frequent usage will assist in creating a rapport with the client.

7. Ask questions that will provide you with essential information to develop a sales proposal.

8. Utilize active listening techniques—rephrasing, restating, summarizing.

9. Take notes—do not rely on your memory to serve you later.

10. Only place the caller on hold if absolutely necessary and check back often to let the caller know that he or she has not been forgotten.

11. Return telephone calls promptly—no later than 24 hours.

12. Thank the caller for calling and assure the caller you want to be of assistance.

Telemarketing allows you to reach a large number of potential users of your product or service in a short amount of time. Typically, the sole objective of the phone call is to secure an appointment, not make the sale; closing a sale normally requires face-to-face contact. Attempting to conduct a sales interview or presentation over the phone is often a waste of time.

A certain rapport must be established prior to trying to arrange an appointment. Your telephone call should include the following steps: greeting, introduction, gratitude, purpose, appointment, and thank you.[2] Do not hesitate to plan and write down what you want to say over the telephone. Doing so will allow you to present a concise, organized message.

Here is a sample opener:

Say: *Good morning, Ms. Porter. I'm Tom Hunt with the Statler Hotel. We provide companies like yours with a broad selection of meeting facilities. I appreciate you giving me a moment of your valuable time. I promise to be brief. If I can show you how to get more out of your company meetings, would you be interested?*

To collect information from this prospect:

Say: *Great, Ms. Porter, but in order to best meet your needs, may I get your response to a couple of questions?*

These questions may provide information about the company background, who makes the buying decisions regarding your services, the prospect's background, desired business terms (direct bill, audiovisual service, etc.), who the prospect presently purchases from, and purchasing policies and practices. You should determine what information will be most crucial to you in assisting the sale prior to placing the telephone call to the prospect.

If at all possible, the goal for these initial calls should also be to arrange an appointment for a face-to-face interview. You can be much more effective as a salesperson when you are face-to-face with the prospect. Rather than asking for an "appointment," which can sound too formal and time-consuming, ask to "visit" or "pop by."[3] If you will be unable to arrange a personal interview, you should seek to get permission to send information and then follow up with another telephone call. Always suggest a specific day and time to meet with the prospect or to make the return phone call.

Don't say: *What would be a convenient time for an appointment?*
Say: *I can arrange my schedule so we can visit on Monday at 1:30 P.M. or would Tuesday at 11:15 A.M. be better?*

Close the phone call with a thank-you, and repeat the time and location of the upcoming meeting. Verify directions if you are unsure of the prospect's whereabouts.

Say: *Thank you for allowing me to visit with you, Ms. Porter. I look forward to meeting you on Monday at 2:15 P.M.*

If enough time will elapse between your phone call and the set appointment, send a professional-looking letter thanking the prospect and confirming the details of the appointment.

Survey Opening
An alternative method of establishing rapport and collecting needed information from a prospective customer is the survey approach.

Say: *Good afternoon, Ms. Rooks. I'm Betty Johnson with ABC Resorts. My firm has asked me to conduct a quick survey involving customer needs. Could you take a few moments to help me?*

If the prospect notes that the timing of your call is bad, apologize and try to get an appointment for a better time. If the prospect agrees to answer your questions, thank her and get right to your questions. The questions should require no more than two minutes of the prospect's time and should be limited to a maximum of five questions. These questions should provide information that helps you qualify the prospect and arouses the curiosity of the prospect regarding your product or service.

Face-to-Face Openings with Prospective Account

If you are able to get face-to-face with a prospect on an initial call, there are several approaches you can use. However, do not imply to the prospect that your visit was just an unplanned afterthought:

Don't say: *Ms. James, I'm Leon Berry with XYZ Inns. I was just passing by and thought I'd drop in and meet you.*

Make certain you provide the prospect with a reason to talk to you.

Say: *Good day, Mr. Berkeley. My name is Jim Merrill and I'm from ABC Resort. I made a special trip today to stop by and introduce myself and my company, and to see if I might be of any assistance to your organization. Can I have a few moments of your time? I promise to be brief.*

OR

Good day. My name is Mary Hendrix. Our company records indicate that we have not successfully earned the opportunity to serve your account. My manager suggested that I personally stop by to introduce myself and make you aware of the changes at our hotel to see if we might earn the right to serve the needs of your organization in the future. Could you spare a few moments?

OR

My name is Ty Watson. I'm with Butler Hotels. The most challenging part of my job is trying to be at the right place at the right time. Unfortunately, I was not able to present my services when you planned your last convention. In order to possibly position my property as a potential convention site, I need your assistance. I assure you that my approach is professional, personal, and to the point. Would you be kind enough to assist me by answering a few questions?

Face-to-Face Openings with Existing Account

Here are some do's and don'ts when you are making a first-time call on a prospect that has previously used your company's services some time in the past:

Don't say: *Mr. Douglas, I'm Ruby Lee with PDQ Inn. I've taken the place of Eric Williams who used to service your account.*

Chances are Mr. Douglas does not know or remember Eric Williams. Furthermore, this opening will not catch Mr. Douglas' attention because it does not suggest that you have something to tell Mr. Douglas that can benefit him.

Say: *Mr. Hubel, I'm Peggy Watts with Hampshire Hotel. There are two reasons I came by today. First, I wanted to let you know that I have replaced Eric Williams, who worked with you in the past, and second, in looking at your account, I've got a couple of ideas I'd like to run by you that could benefit your firm.*

OR

Ms. Hartsfield, I'm Keith Jacobs with the Lord Henry Inn. A few months ago we provided your company with meeting facilities. If this is a good time, I'd like to let you know about a special rate we have developed for businesses like yours, and a few other items that may be of interest.

Follow these openings with:

and first, to make sure I'm making the best recommendations, I'd like to update my files here on what you need . . .

These openings help put your customer at ease because you are letting that person know that you are truly interested in learning what his or her needs are. Consequently, the potential buyer is more likely to share information with you.

Other Opening Methods

Air of Mystery. An "air of mystery or curiosity" opening is designed to get the prospect's attention without specifically identifying the product, service, or plan to be sold.

I have an opportunity for you today that on average has increased the sales of our customers by 20 percent. This approach gets the buyer to focus on what you will say next.

Service. A "service" opening is a promise to help the prospect save time or improve efficiency by doing a job that person might normally have to do.

I'll see that your travel itinerary and tickets are hand delivered to you and your employees each time a booking is made with our firm.

A service opening helps the prospective buyer visualize a short- or long-term gain for his or her operation by allowing you to assist in a specific idea.

Idea. An "idea" opening gains the prospect's attention with a thought or plan that will improve his or her operation.

You will improve employee morale and productivity by awarding weekend stays at our resort for your top three salespeople and their families. Let me show you some letters I have from other satisfied corporate customers.

An idea opening gets the prospective buyer's attention because that person believes that such action will benefit him or her.

Name or Referral. A "name or referral" opening gives credibility to the product, service, or plan because someone the prospect respects supports it.

I was speaking with Sue Smith at XYZ Electronics yesterday and she mentioned that you might be interested in our new three-day cruises.

The use of a name or referral approach adds reassurance that somebody else supports the proposal. Merely addressing the buyer by her given name is not a Name or Referral opening. Also consider having a satisfied customer set up the appointment with the prospect or having the satisfied customer write a letter to the prospect introducing you and your company. You may even want to schedule a lunch where you, the satisfied customer, and the prospect can meet. If you choose to pursue this latter option, just be sure that you will be able to accomplish your sales objectives and will not be simply engaging in small talk.

Benefit or End Result. A "benefit or end result" opening gains the prospective buyer's attention by identifying the specific benefit that can be realized as a result of your proposal.

You will be able to devote more time to your business and your customers by simply letting our full-service staff handle the many minute details of your annual awards banquet. We can provide you with a hassle-free, stellar event.

A benefit or end result opening focuses the prospect's attention on real gains as a result of the action.

Startling Statement. A "startling statement" opening is the positioning of something factual in a dramatic way to arouse the prospect's attention.

You have lost at least $10 on every room reservation you made this year by not taking advantage of our special corporate membership!

A startling statement opening focuses the prospective buyer's attention on a lost opportunity.

Recognition or Compliment. A "recognition or compliment" opening is your acknowledgment of the prospect's professional approach and understanding of the business.

You are a highly respected member of the business community, so we would like to extend you the first invitation to join our new Windstar Country Club.

A recognition or compliment opening says to the prospect: "You are somebody!"

Product. A "product" opening demonstrates product benefits and features.

Greater conference attendance results in a more profitable, successful event. Let me show you how our meeting room facilities and other amenities can increase participation in your conference

A product opening grasps the prospective buyer's attention quickly.

Question. A "question" opening is designed to motivate the prospective buyer to respond in a positive manner.

Mrs. Jones, are you interested in saving money on your business travel?

A question approach involves the prospect in the selling process.

 ## Openings Exercise

Take 15 minutes and write an opening statement that you can use for each of these types of openings. As you prepare these openings, think about the social style that would be most receptive to each type.

Telephone Approach

_____

_____

_____

Telephone Survey Method

_____

_____

_____

Face-to-Face with New Prospect

_____

_____

_____

_____

Face-to-Face with Current Account

_____

_____

_____

Air of Mystery or Curiosity

_____

_____

_____

Service

_____

_____

_____

Idea

_____

_____

_____

Name or Referral

_____

_____

_____

Benefit or End Result

_____

_____

_____

Startling Statement

_____

_____

_____

Recognition or Compliment

_____

_____

_____

Product

_____

_____

_____

Question

_____

_____

_____

If you found that creating the openings in the Openings Exercise required more effort and time than you thought it would, then you should recognize that openings require planning. If you just walk into a prospect's office and blurt out the first thing that comes to mind, you will not likely be uttering the best possible opening. Remember, there is only one chance to a make a first impression, so make it a good one.

If you have used an effective opening, you should now have the prospect's attention. Once you have the prospective buyer's attention, however, that attention must be directed quickly to the prospect's needs that your product or service will satisfy. Therefore, it is imperative that you move directly into the interest stage and present reason-to-buy statements. The link between your opening and the first reason-to-buy statement should be logical and flow naturally.

SPIN Opening

Another very effective opening approach is the **SPIN** technique.[4] SPIN stands for **S**ituation, **P**roblem, **I**mplication, and **N**eed-payoff. SPIN requires asking a series of questions to quickly develop rapport, collect information, and illustrate that you are interested in meeting the customer's needs. This method provides an excellent opening and also gains the prospect's permission to move directly into your presentation. Although a SPIN opening requires some practice on your part to learn it, the benefits gained are well worth the effort. You will find this opening one of the most effective you can use.

Situation questions are those concerning the prospect's general business situation as it relates to your product. These questions are fairly broad and provide a general understanding of the prospect's needs or problems, so that you can smoothly transition into questions on specific areas. Think of these as warm-up questions.

Problem questions ask about specific needs, difficulties, or dissatisfactions the prospect may be experiencing that you may be able to solve. The goal here is to have the prospect recognize and admit that there is a problem. You must determine which of the prospect's problems are important enough that the prospect will be willing to do something about it. This information can be used to focus on the areas that are of special interest to your prospect.

Implication questions ask how a specific problem affects the prospect's home, life, or business operations. The objective of asking these implication questions is to get the prospect to realize that the problem may have a broader impact than previously thought. If possible, use bottom-line figures or statistics in the implication question.

Need-payoff questions are similar to benefit statements. The prospect has identified the problem for you, so you must simply tie in the benefit. "If I can show you how to take care of this problem (naming specific issue), then would you be interested?" If you get a positive response, you can move into your sales presentation. If you get a negative response from the prospect, begin the problem, implication, and need-payoff questions again. This latter situation may occur if you fail to establish that this particular need is really important to the prospect.

When using a SPIN opening, it is essential that you identify problems and implications that are important to the prospective buyer. If you use a need-payoff question, but obtain a negative response from the prospect, you have failed to identify a need that is of sufficient importance to the prospect. As a result, the prospect does not feel compelled to take the action you want that person to take. When this situation occurs, you must recycle back to the problem and implication questions and continue repeating the SPIN steps until a pressing need is identified. When you have revealed an important problem or a crucial implication has surfaced that the prospect has not previously considered, you will obtain a positive response to the need-payoff question.

Identifying SPIN Questions Exercise

Read through the following sales-call transcript and identify the different types of SPIN questions that were used to uncover the prospect's needs. Place your answer in the column marked Question Category. Remember, there are four basic types of questions:

Situation Questions	General data-gathering questions about background and current facts that are very broad in nature.
Problem Questions	Questions about specific difficulties, problems or dissatisfactions experienced by the prospect.
Implication Questions	Questions that logically follow one or more problem questions that are designed to help the prospect recognize the true ramification of the problem.
Need-Payoff Questions	Questions that ask about the usefulness of solving a problem.

Situation. The salesperson is selling room nights and catering services to the manager of a large natural gas facility.

		SPIN Question Category
Seller:	Thanks for allowing me to visit with you today. I've heard this is a busy time of year for you. Is that correct?	_____
Buyer:	That's right. It takes a lot of hard work and preparation.	
Seller:	I understand and I'll be brief. How often do you have plant get-togethers, like picnics, parties, and banquets?	_____
Buyer:	We have a holiday party in December, but our big event is each fall when we hold our Safety Banquet. This event is to celebrate our completion of an entire year without a lost-time accident.	

		SPIN Question Category

Seller:	How many people usually attend these events?	_____
Buyer:	About 250 attend the Safety Banquet—that's our big event. Employees and their spouses attend, and many executives from our headquarters fly in for the event. We usually get some rooms at a nearby hotel and then have a big banquet at a nice restaurant in town. The banquet emphasizes safety to our employees, and helps build loyalty to our company.	
Seller:	Who usually organizes and caters your banquet?	_____
Buyer:	We organize it! The restaurant, of course, provides the food that we order.	
Seller:	Are you happy with the arrangement?	_____
Buyer:	Yes and no. It's a pretty cheap way to do it, but sometimes our staff just can't seem to create the special feel that the evening is supposed to have. They try, but heaven knows they're not the most creative bunch when it comes to themes and decorations.	
Seller:	Do your guests that are staying in the hotel ever have trouble finding the location of the restaurant in town? For example, do some of the executives get lost and arrive late to the banquet?	_____
Buyer:	Sure, some times things do get mixed up at the last minute. We try to leave maps at the hotel for the executives, but they don't always get them.	
Seller:	Does this lead to anxiety for your staff?	_____
Buyer:	Yes! And for me as well! I don't want my boss driving all over town looking for the restaurant. Besides, I want these events to come off without a hitch, so my employees feel special. My employees work hard all year long. This banquet is an opportunity to say "Thank you for another great year" and "We're a great team." When something doesn't go as planned, I sure run through the antacid tablets!	
Seller:	If I can show you a way to reduce that stress would you be interested?	_____
Buyer:	Not if its going to cost me a lot of money! Let's face it, bottles of Rolaids are cheap compared to paying somebody big bucks just to make sure the guests arrive on time.	
Seller:	Earlier you mentioned creativity. I'm sure your staff is outstanding in the way it executes day-to-day operations here at the plant, but you indicated that you thought your staff was lacking in creativity for your annual Safety Banquet. Is that right?	_____
Buyer:	Yeah, it is hard for them to come up with new ideas each year.	

		SPIN Question Category
Seller:	As a result, do you think that you are able to produce the full benefits of your banquets when they lack the creativity you are seeking?	_____
Buyer:	What are you driving at?	
Seller:	Well, does the theme for your banquet arouse excitement and motivation? Do your employees get pumped up about attending the banquet? Do they act in a more positive manner after the get-together?	_____
Buyer:	No, not really.	
Seller:	So, if I understand correctly, you are saying that the annual Safety Banquet may not generate all of the long-term benefits you've been seeking. Is that right?	_____
Buyer:	Yeah. I'm not sure the Safety Banquets have resulted in happier or more motivated employees who work harder and smarter.	
Seller:	If I can show you a way to generate excitement about the Safety Banquet and to facilitate an increase in employee productivity afterwards, would you be interested?	_____
Buyer:	Yes, I would definitely like to know how to do that.	

 ## SPIN Role-Play Exercise

Practice SPIN with a friend by performing the following role-play exercise. Assume you are working in sales for a conference hotel. You are meeting for the first time with Mr. Turner, director of the National Wholesalers Association (NWA). He is in charge of planning the Association's annual three-day meeting, which has typically been held on a local campus during the slower summer months. Mr. Turner feels that he saves NWA money by utilizing dorms for hotel rooms and classrooms for meeting rooms.

You have learned that NWA is a large association of companies, of various size, that represents more than 15 different industries. The members who participate in NWA meetings hold top management positions—including owners, CEOs, and presidents—within their respective firms and range in age from 45-70, with the majority in their late 50s to early 60s. The members pay annual dues to the association, but the association's largest fund-raising event is this annual meeting.

Utilize SPIN and active listening techniques to develop a rapport, gather information, and get the prospect to agree to listen to your presentation regarding booking this annual event.

Key Concepts

A good opening is crucial to grabbing the attention of the prospect. In this chapter, the main points regarding openings are:

- Openings should gain the attention of the prospect, arouse interest in the salesperson's proposal, and allow the salesperson to gain control of the interaction. Good openings will determine how receptive prospects are, how difficult or easy the close will be, and how welcome the salesperson will be on follow-up visits.

- Good openings specify owner benefits that appeal to a specific need or want of the prospective buyer.

- Openings include telephone openings, survey openings, face-to-face openings with existing accounts, face-to-face openings with prospective accounts. Other openings include the air of mystery opening, service opening, idea opening, name or referral opening, benefit or end result opening, startling statement opening, recognition or compliment opening, product opening, and question opening.

- SPIN opening combines opening and probing. The steps in SPIN involve situation questions, problems questions, implication questions, and need-payoff questions. Although a more advance sales technique, SPIN is one of the most effective opening methods.

Endnotes

[1] Adapted from Feiertag, Howard (1991), "Collect Information to Close Telephone Inquiries," *Hotel and Motel Management* 206 (November 4), 1; Feiertag, Howard (1992), "Mishandled Inquiries Are Lost Opportunities," *Hotel and Motel Management* 207 (March 23), 17; Feiertag, Howard (1993), "Rig Up More Business by Improving Phone Procedures," *Hotel and Motel Management* 208 (August 16), 13; Feiertag, Howard (1998), "How Much Business Did You Lose Today?" *Hotel and Motel Management* 213 (March 2), 58; Cronin, Ralph M. (1997), "The Telephone—Salesperson's Friend or Foe?" *The American Salesman* 42 (November), 23-28.

[2] Hopkins, Tom (1995), *Selling for Dummies*, Foster City, CA: IDG Books Worldwide.

[3] Hopkins, Tom (1995), *Selling for Dummies*, Foster City, CA: IDG Books Worldwide.

[4] To learn more about SPIN, see Rackham, Neil (1998), *Spin Selling*, New York: McGraw-Hill.

6

PROBING FOR NEEDS

People find themselves in selling situations every day, not just at work, but in many other environments. For example, as a child, you may have tried to "sell" your parents on the value of a new toy or as a teenager you may have attempted to "sell" your parents on a later curfew. More recently, you may have tried to "sell" a friend or significant other on seeing a particular movie or vacation destination. You may have sought to convince a prospective employer that you are the best job candidate, or you may have tried to negotiate a raise with your current employer. Occasionally, however, you may have been disappointed that your spouse, friend, or boss did not accept your idea. After these encounters, have you ever attempted to determine why your idea was rejected by another individual or why your offer of service was not accepted?

Approaches to Selling

The matter of selling or convincing another person to accept one's ideas, services or plans is an integral part of most jobs. There are many ways in which one individual can convince another. Best known, of course, is the "hard sell" approach, which often comes through as commanding or "giving directions." However, many people in business today are experimenting with approaches other than the "hard sell," such as the consultative selling approach introduced in the first chapter of this book. The consultive selling approach is based on the quality of the salesperson's idea, expertise or competence, and/or personal relationships. The need to sell and convince through the power of an idea or competence is becoming more crucial as more professionals enter the business world, and people are less impressed by a domineering, fast-talking personality.

Short- and long-term benefits are derived by applying this more professional, consultative approach. For the short term, the seller and buyer are better able to reach a mutual agreement on implementing the idea, service, or plan. As each mutually agreed-upon idea is implemented and obtains the desired result, the buyer and seller begin to develop a personal relationship. The degree to which a quality personal relationship evolves will be contingent upon the salesperson's ability to influence the buyer through the power of the salesperson's offering. Inherent in a quality personal relationship is the long-term benefit for both buyer and seller—the buyer recognizes that the salesperson is indeed interested in the buyer's business, and the salesperson has demonstrated the ability to satisfy the buyer's needs. That is, the salesperson must demonstrate the ability to be a problem solver. As a result of building a quality personal relationship, the long-term benefit for the salesperson lies in the increased likelihood of the buyer's acceptance of future proposals. By building a quality personal relationship, the salesperson will have established a bond with the buyer that is necessary to consummate the sales transaction.

As a salesperson, you should seek to identify the needs of the other person, including both organizational and personal needs. Too often, ideas are presented from the frame of reference of the "seller," rather than from the needs of the individual or group concerned. A prospective buyer wants to be treated as unique, and to be recognized for particular differences. Probing for the prospective buyer's needs followed by listening, restating, or summarizing the prospect's position are ways to become more influential. This kind of "persuasive strategy" is in direct opposition to the "hard sell" approach, which tends to make people defensive, and to lead them away from acceptance.

Gaining the Prospect's Involvement and Participation

Through the process of listening and probing, you can encourage the prospect's participation and/or involvement in planning and identifying needs. The prospect's involvement in the sales process helps to establish an atmosphere of openness to exchange information and feelings. In turn, this leads to a relationship of trust and confidence, making suggestions, and following through on recommendations. Consequently, it is more likely that the prospect will become committed to whatever agreements are reached.

To gain an understanding of the prospect's needs and to get the prospect emotionally involved in the sales process, you must ask questions or "probe." When asking questions, keep in mind these four simple rules:

1. Don't ask questions that might lead to situations from which you cannot escape.

2. Ask only one question at a time.

3. Allow prospects time to answer each question.

4. Listen—concentrate on what the buyer is saying.

Probing for Needs

A prospect's decision-making process can be affected by his or her organization's needs or by personal needs. Although buyers buy benefits, they tend to be more apt to buy benefits that will satisfy specific organizational needs. In any sales situation, three kinds of needs most likely will emerge:

Financial	Refers to maintaining or improving monetary results; controlling costs.
Image	Refers to maintaining or improving prestige or credibility.
Performance	Refers to maintaining or improving productivity.

Classifying and identifying needs can be helpful in the following ways:

1. to understand the rationale behind a buyer's decision and what motivates the buyer to buy

2. to establish a direction for planning and conducting the sales call

3. to identify and apply benefits that satisfy specific organizational or personal needs

There are really just two basic sources of information regarding the prospect's needs. First, the buyer, in a conversation with you, will give information allowing you to conclude what organizational or personal needs are important to him or her. Second, people associated with the account—other salespeople, people writing in trade publications about the account, financial journals, or reports about the account—all give information that may relate to the prospect's organizational needs.

Needs are frequently interrelated and can influence each other. Consider Company C that wants to improve its bottom-line profit, and still wants to maintain the company's high quality image. The result of satisfying one need might also create or intensify another. Therefore, it is important not only to appeal to the prospect's specific needs, but to be cognizant of the proposal's implications on the other needs. Ultimately, your ability to recognize and understand a prospect's needs, and then to satisfy them with the appropriate benefits are key factors in the prospective buyer's decision to buy.

Types of Probing Questions

Probing questions can be placed into four categories: **closed**, **open-ended**, **directive**, and **reflective**. These questions can be used alone or in combination with one another.

Closed questions can be answered with only a few words, such as yes or no. These types of questions are not very effective in developing customer needs because the answers provide little information. For this reason, you should use closed questions sparingly. In their place, learn to employ open-ended questions.

Open-ended questions cannot be answered with a simple yes or no. These questions invite a true expression of opinion and feeling regardless of whether they are favorable or unfavorable to your perspective. This type of question frequently asks who, what, where, when, why, and how. The purpose of open-ended questions is to elicit information from the prospect. You should use open-ended questions frequently.

For example:

> What do you think of . . . ?
> Where could you use . . . ?
> How do you feel about . . . ?
> What is most important to you regarding . . . ?

Directive questions are those that request expansion or further explanation of one particular point. Generally speaking, you should use these questions to get the buyer to concentrate on the parts of your proposal with which he or she feels more comfortable or agreeable. The more you get the prospect to explore the areas of agreement, the less important the areas of disagreement will seem. Further, directive questions help you to reestablish positive communication after a negative response from the prospect. Use directive questions frequently.

Reflective questions are used to clarify the prospect's meaning and to determine needs. The reflective question can be used to buy you some "thinking" time when the prospect has presented a surprise objection. Reflection means the repetition or rephrasing in your own words, of what the other person is trying to say or seems to feel. Therefore, the first essential to reflection is careful listening and the second is selectivity. To properly reflect the prospect's feelings, you must really listen to the prospect and not be thinking about your own plan or what you are going to say next. Then, you have to select the most important idea or feeling from what was said and put it into your own words. Use reflective questions sparingly.

Open-ended, directive, and reflective questions may be used to not only elicit information from prospective buyers, but to respond to objections. That is, sometimes using questions to probe further will provide the key to overcoming a prospect's objection. For example:

Buyer:	"Your price is too high."
Salesperson:	"Why do you feel the price is too high?"

OR

Buyer:	"Does your resort allow children?"
Salesperson:	"Why is that important to you?"

Open-Ended Questions Exercise

Instructions: Below you are provided with several buying situations. Respond with an open-ended question in the space provided. Take five minutes to complete the exercise.

1. Buyer: *"I don't like your proposal."*

    You could say: _____

    _____

2. Buyer: *"Gosh, I think your ideas are terrific, but to tell you the truth, the boss just can't see doing something new like this. I don't think he would buy it."*

    You could say: _____

    _____

3. Buyer: *"I don't know. I'll have to think it over."*

    You could say: _____

    _____

4. Buyer: *"I'll have to talk to someone else about it."*

    You could say: _____

    _____

Directive Questions Exercise

Instructions: Below you are provided with several buyer reactions. Respond with a **directive question** in the space provided. Take five minutes to complete the exercise.

1. Buyer: *"Gosh, I think your ideas are terrific, but to tell you the truth, the boss just can't see doing something new like this. I don't think he would buy it."*

   You could say: _____

   _____

2. Buyer: *"I like your remodeled rooms, but they cost too much."*

   You could say: _____

   _____

3. Buyer: *"That's a good room rate, but your banquet service prices are too high."*

   You could say: _____

   _____

4. Buyer: *"A new corporate program, eh? It's about time you guys came up with something new. See me in three months and we can talk it over then."*

   You could say: _____

   _____

Reflective Exercise

Instructions: Below you are provided with several buyer reactions. Respond with a **reflective question** in the space provided. Take five minutes to complete the exercise.

1. Buyer: *"There's certainly a lot to be said for your plan, but I'd like to think it over and get back to you."*

   You could say: _____

   _____

2. Buyer: *"Anyone can find reasons for changing, however before we start using your hotel for all our business travel, you have to present me with significant reasons for doing so."*

   You could say: _____

   _____

3. Buyer: *"You know, I've been in the business a long time, and I've heard the same old story from you guys for many years."*

You could say: _____

_____

4. Buyer: *"Your proposal is great for the big company, but my company needs are entirely different."*

You could say: _____

_____

 Utilizing Probing Role-Playing Exercise

Seller's Role

Your task is to prepare for a three-minute sales presentation to a buyer for a hospitality product. You should take eight to ten minutes to prepare the presentation and close the sale. The objective of this exercise is for you to practice the questioning techniques discussed as a means to influence a buyer to buy, and to close the sale.

You will be rated by an observer according to the following scale:

1. Four points for each open-ended or directive question.

2. Five points for each reflection statement.

3. Five bonus points if you close the sale.

Buyer's Role

Your role is to be the recipient of a sales presentation. The objective of the exercise is to give the salesperson the opportunity to practice the questioning techniques learned in the chapter. Encourage the salesperson to ask open-ended questions by refusing to elaborate when asked a closed-ended question. That is, answer a closed-ended question with only "yes," "no" or the specific data requested. An observer will score the performance of the salesperson.

Your task is to buy, if the salesperson convinces you to do so. As evidence of your conviction, you will "pay" the salesperson for the product. Pay can be nominal, such as a candy bar.

Observer's Role

Your role is to observe a sales presentation for a hospitality product to be delivered by one of your fellow participants in the role playing to another participant who will be playing the role of a buyer.

Your task is to identify how many times the salesperson uses each of the questioning techniques studied. You will keep score (see the score sheet in Figure 6-1) according to the following scale:

1. Four points for each open-ended or directive question.

2. Five points for each reflection statement.

3. Five bonus points if the salesperson closes the sale.

Open-ended	Directive	Reflection	Incorrect Use or Poor Listening Technique
1.			
2.			
3.			
4.			
5.			
6.			
7.			
8.			
9.			
10.			

Did the salesperson close the sale?   Yes_____   No_____

Figure 6-1 Probing Questions Role Playing Score Sheet

Key Concepts

Probing helps the salesperson identify the needs of the prospect, so that the salesperson can serve as a problem solver. Chapter 6 has discussed the concept of probing and its importance in the sales process. The following are the key points of this chapter:

◆ Continuous probing throughout the sales process maintains the prospect's involvement and ensures that the prospect is in agreement with the salesperson's proposal.

◆ Probing allows the salesperson to understand the rationale and motivation behind a prospect's decision, establishes a direction for the sales call, and identifies benefits that satisfy specific needs.

◆ Probing questions are categorized as closed, open-ended, directive, and reflective. Closed questions should be used sparingly; open-ended questions should be used frequently. Directive questions emphasize a positive point made by the prospect, while reflective questions rephrase or restate the prospect's comments. The latter two types of questions should be used only when warranted.

THE PRESENTATION

A s noted in previous chapters, your job as a salesperson is to be a problem solver for the buyer. Through problem solving, you create value for the buyer and encourage a long-term relationship. Chapter 7 explains the difference between owner benefits and product characteristics, and teaches the use of reason-to-buy statements that are focused on resolving the prospect's problems. Also described are the progression of owner benefits with the focus on "higher order" benefits reflecting the greatest importance to the prospect. Next discussed is the creation of win-win situations for the salesperson and the buyer through the use of presentations customized to include the benefits desired by each buyer. Finally, tips and techniques for improving oral communication skills and poise are presented.

Owner Benefit Plus Product Characteristic: Developing the Reason-to-Buy Statement

An **owner benefit** is a gain for the buyer that results when the product, service, or plan the salesperson has proposed is put to use. Owner benefits answer the buyer's question: *What's in it for me?* Owner benefits are determined by the needs and wants of the buyer.

A **product characteristic** is an individual part of a product, service, or plan, and the way in which the parts are integrated. Product characteristics are always part of the product, whether the product is used or not. Product characteristics are always the source of owner benefits.

People buy, not because of characteristics the product has to offer, but to obtain the benefits that the characteristics can produce. For example, if you purchased an automobile with an air conditioner, you likely did so because it would provide you with the benefit of keeping you cool during the warm summer months so your clothes and hair would not be stuck to your skin, and in turn, you could appear more polished. Professional salespeople should analyze the prospective buyer's needs and offer benefits that will satisfy those needs. When a salesperson offers an owner benefit, the salesperson is actually promising a future gain or improvement because benefits come to a buyer only after he or she accepts or purchases the product, service, or plan offered.

For this reason, a buyer often questions a salesperson's statement of owner benefits. The buyer wants to know the source—how or why the benefit is possible. As the source is always a characteristic, the combination of owner benefit and product characteristic makes a forceful and effective reason-to-buy statement. When possible, state the owner benefit first, followed by the product characteristic. Reason-to-buy statements (owner benefits plus product characteristics) are important because:

1. The statement is buyer-oriented.

2. Product characteristics clarify owner benefits.

3. Product characteristics support owner benefits.

Examples of Reason-to-Buy Statements:

Sales manager to corporate meeting planner:
> "The sales force of your corporation will be energized and motivated to sell more if you use our state-of-the-art, executive theater to conduct your new product meetings."

Catering manager to client:
> "Your dinner guests will be awed by the spectacular view provided by this private dining room."

 # Owner Benefits/Product Characteristics Exercise

Underline the owner benefits twice and the product characteristics once in each one of the statements listed below.

Example:

Sales Representative to Manager:
> "Mr. Sweeney, you will <u>increase your participation</u> and <u>bring more customers into your trade show</u> when you <u>utilize our centrally located convention center</u>."

1. Sales Representative to Association Director:
> "You can ensure rave reviews by using our 'Hall of Mirrors' Ballroom for your banquet."

2. Sales Representative to Manager:
> "You will increase traffic at your booth if you provide complimentary coffee to trade show attendees."

3. Salesperson to Convention Planner:
> "Mr. Johnson, you can eliminate participant confusion and increase session participation by televising the session agenda throughout the hotel."

4. Sales Representative to Manager:
> "You can reduce your company's business travel expenses by utilizing our hotel with its complimentary breakfast."

5. Sales Representative to Future Bride:

"Ms. Smith, you won't be embarrassed about running low on hors d'oeuvres at your wedding reception if you request our automatic refill service."

6. Salesperson to Convention Planner:

"Increasing the entree table by three feet will reduce out-of-stocks and speed buffet service for all your guests. "

7. Sales Representative to Corporate Manager:

"Your company will save money and your out-of-town employees will be more comfortable during long stays using our furnished corporate apartments."

Progression of Owner Benefits

A progression of owner benefits (POB) is a process for examining how an owner benefit, which the buyer initially derives because of a particular product characteristic, can produce other owner benefits. Thus, one owner benefit can produce another owner benefit that produces yet another benefit, and so on. This process of developing the progression of owner benefits allows you to determine how your product may be leading to higher-order benefits or benefits that are more meaningful to the customer. In addition, the process requires that you consider how each characteristic of your product or service might benefit the owner. Consequently, your recognition of all the benefits your product can provide, directly or indirectly, expands significantly and assists you in preparing stronger reason-to-buy statements. The following example demonstrates how one POB might appear:

Example of Progression of Owner Benefits

Service:	Complimentary buffet breakfast for corporate clients
Characteristic:	Spread of food available within the hotel over a broad time period at no cost.
First Use:	Free breakfast can be readily consumed within the hotel with no wait time.

Owner Benefit

O.B. #1	Saves guest time	Low Order O.B.
O.B. #2	Guest can sleep later	↓
O.B. #3	Guest is more rested	↓
O.B. #4	Guest is more productive	↓
O.B. #5	Corporate productivity increases	↓
O.B. #6	Corporation makes more money	↓
O.B. #7	Increased profits result in higher pay	↓
O.B. #8	Better standard of living for guest	High Order O.B.

When developing your own POB, there is a set of steps to follow:

Step 1.   Study the product characteristics of your offering (product, service, or plan).

Step 2.   Identify the one product characteristic you want to analyze. There are likely other characteristics in which you are interested, but each one should be examined separately.

Step 3.   Determine the first use of the product characteristic. This is the first thing that happens when the product characteristic goes into use. You may find that there is more than one first use of the characteristic. If so, develop a separate POB for each.

Step 4.   Develop additional owner benefits from the product characteristic's first use that you chose.

Step 5.   Proceed with the POB. Each subsequent owner benefit in the POB should be a logical result of the previously stated owner benefit.

A simple way to search for the subsequent owner benefit is to ask, "What results from this?" or state the owner benefit, followed by "therefore," which will lead you to the next logical owner benefit. The resulting owner benefit should be a natural outgrowth of the already stated owner benefit.

To check if you have skipped any steps ask: "Why is this possible?" If the natural answer is the previously stated owner benefit, your development is logical and believable.

You may come to a point where you can see more than one owner benefit logically resulting from an owner benefit already stated. For instance, look at the buffet breakfast example again:

Characteristic: Spread of food available within the hotel over a broad time period at no cost.
First Use: Free breakfast can be readily consumed within the hotel with no wait time.

At this point in the POB, you have more than one way to go. For example, rather than *saves time*, you could choose *saves money*.

When faced with this situation, select one of the owner benefits and complete the progression. Then, come back and take each of the other owner benefits in turn and go through the analysis again.

When developing a POB on paper, always begin with a product characteristic of your product, service, or plan. However, when using the POB in the actual sales presentation, always *state the owner benefit with the most credibility and meaning to the prospect first, then work your way back to the product characteristic and product.*

High-Order/Low-Order Owner Benefits

The owner benefit with the most meaning to the *prospect* is the **highest order benefit**. The owner benefit that results from the product characteristic's first use is a **low order benefit**. Choosing the most powerful and credible benefit to meet your prospect's need reduces the risk of losing the sale.

As with benefits, there are high-order and low-order product characteristics. When developing a POB, choose a high-order product characteristic that will lead logically to high-order owner benefits that will meet your buyer's needs. Avoid developing POB that are overloaded with "hairsplitting" owner benefits. Use only those required to make the POB logical and meaningful to the prospect.

The progression of owner benefits (POB) process is invaluable in analyzing your product, service, or plan, and in preparing a sales presentation. In addition, the process makes it possible to develop a complete line of reasoning that can be relayed to the prospect to not only persuade, but to educate, what your offering can do for the prospect. After presenting logical reason-to-buy statements, ensure that the buyer is in agreement by asking, "How does that sound?" or "What do you think of that?" Use the Progression of Benefits Summary Sheet as a planning tool.

PROGRESSION OF BENEFITS (SUMMARY SHEET)

Use this as a planning tool.

Think of your product:

1. List the product characteristics.

2. Choose one product characteristic that is:
   a. unique to your product/service or
   b. different for your product/service.

3. Think of your customer(s).
   For example:
   > Business travelers
   > Leisure travelers
   > Conventions and groups

4. With your customer(s) in mind:
   develop a POB for the product characteristic. Make sure it is
   logical, believable, and easily understood from where he or she stands.

5. Check your POB:
   Does the POB lead logically, believably, and easily, to a real need or want
   of that buyer?

   If not: Choose another product characteristic and repeat steps two and three above until you find a product characteristic that gives you the answer to four above.
   If yes: In your presentation, first use the benefit discovered that best meets the need or want of the buyer. Build the presentation from there.

Progression of Owner Benefits Work Sheet

Progression of owner benefits means that the owner benefits accrue to the buyer because of the existence of a particular characteristic of your product. A POB *grows from other* owner benefits. Using the following template, practice creating a POB.

Progression of Owner Benefits

Product: _____

Characteristic: _____

Progression of O.B.s

O.B. #1 _____

O.B. #2 _____

O.B. #3 _____

O.B. #4 _____

O.B. #5 _____

O.B. #6 _____

O.B. #7 _____

O.B. #8 _____

Creating Win-Win Situations Exercise

In a successful sale *everyone wins*. However, you must identify how each buyer on your customer map can personally win from what you have to offer. Using the space that follows, write down the name of each buyer on your customer map (see Chapter 2). Then, next to each customer's name, write down what direct benefit this buyer will obtain from your product and then what personal win the buyer will receive. A personal win, for example, could be increased recognition at work or greater free time. Once again, if you don't know the benefit or win each buyer is seeking, you should denote this as a red flag, and make it your business to learn the personal needs of each buyer.[1]

Name of Buyer	Benefit of Your Product	Personal Win for Buyer

Effective Oral Communication Skills

Have you ever had the experience of telling a story and by the time it circles back to you many of the facts have been eliminated or distorted? The same thing can happen when you make a presentation to one prospect who then relays it to others in the prospect's company. What can you do to improve understanding, so that the facts are not forgotten or mixed up? You can strengthen the presentation by taking steps to keep the buyer's attention, improve the buyer's understanding, help the buyer remember what was said, and create a sense of value.

Oral Delivery

How you say something is just as important as what you say in making your presentation. The oral delivery of a presentation is one of the most critical factors that affect the buyer's interest and perception of the benefits of the proposal. This statement also suggests the buyer's decision will be influenced by the seller's oral delivery. A well-prepared presentation that is poorly delivered, seldom results in an acceptance of the proposal. However, a seller who delivers that same presentation and adds life and energy to it by stressing and emphasizing the key benefits improves the likelihood of the proposal's acceptance. Furthermore, the quality and style with which the presentation is delivered can add vitality and excitement to a less interesting topic or proposal.

By recalling some of the speakers to whom you have listened, you will have an illustration of how oral delivery can affect the listener. Some speakers have the ability or skill to take absolutely dry subject matter and deliver it in a fashion that makes the material interesting and the learning process easy. Conversely, other people, because of their poor oral delivery, will make an exciting topic seem less interesting or even boring.

As listeners, the degree of interest in the content material frequently changes, not on the basis of the content itself, but, instead, on the oral delivery of the presentation. This then implies that oral delivery has a significant impact on the degree of the listeners' interests, and how well they receive the message. For salespeople, it means that they must not only be aware of this fact, but must also employ skillful techniques to ensure that their oral delivery enhances the presentation.

The ability of a professional salesperson to deliver an effective oral presentation adds another dimension to the diverse, yet interrelated, skills necessary to succeed in today's environment. Each of these skills plays an integral role in determining the final outcome of the presentation. Therefore, it is of paramount importance for salespeople to employ good techniques in order to improve their oral delivery of a presentation.

The Effective Oral Presentation

Energize. The first step in developing effective oral sales talks is to learn how to energize presentations to motivate your customers. In speaking to others, interest is maintained in part through the energy of the communication. Unfortunately, there is a natural tendency to reduce the level of emotion when someone is apprehensive. This tendency suppresses energy and makes a presentation less interesting. Explore ways of harnessing and converting nervous energy and inhibition into positive energy that can dramatically change the way you communicate. You should sit or stand comfortably, but firmly. You will use this base as a launching pad for releasing your energy. Next, consciously raise the volume of your voice when you present. Raise your voice level by about 25 percent above a conversational level to increase your intensity and to release nervous energy. The raising of voice volume also raises the presenter's energy level and releases emotion to supplement the message. The increased energy level tends to generate body movement and gestures to support the presenter's message. As the speaker is energized, so, in turn, are the listeners.

Generate Interest. Second, explore ways of heightening your listeners' interest, and of being more effective and assured. Examine the ways your body language can be used to communicate and identify specific techniques for making your presentations more interesting. Leave your arms and hands free and relaxed in a comfortable position, so that your gestures develop naturally from your enthusiasm and vocal emphasis. Lean slightly toward the customers and gesture toward them.

Next, learn some basic vocal techniques that can add assurance to your presentations. "Punch out" or emphasize key words to provide impact and authority. Also, examine and use techniques for establishing more effective rapport through eye contact. Research indicates that salespeople who use effective eye contact are much more successful, and that good eye contact is also a key factor in establishing credibility and a feeling of friendship with a customer.[2] If the customer perceives you as friendly, you will be twice as successful in selling the product. To establish appropriate eye contact, first focus your attention and your eyes totally on the customer. Hold eye contact with him or her for three to five seconds and do not break it to look around. Only break eye contact by blinking, but be cautioned that intense staring, without blinking, can be interpreted as aggressive behavior. The intensity of eye contact is enhanced through facial gestures, such as smiling and other gestures of friendliness, including empathy, concern, and understanding. If possible, videotape yourself practicing a sales presentation or have a friend observe you. Watch to see if you are using these distracting eye patterns: (1) scanning—looking around the room while you are talking, (2) framing—looking up or down when deciding what to say next, or (3) darting—moving your eyes around in a quick, nervous fashion. If you find yourself incorporating these poor eye techniques, work at getting rid of them.

Address Needs. Third, use a systematic approach for targeting oral and written presentations to the needs of individual customers. Utilize a cycle of probing, listening, responding, and verifying agreement. That is, ask a probing, open-ended question; listen carefully to the expressed needs of the prospect; respond by rephrasing the need, identifying a solution, and tying it to the features of your product or service; ensure the buyer agrees with your solution; then proceed with another probing question. For example:

Salesperson:	*Tell me, what are the most critical attributes that will determine where you will conduct your meeting?*
Buyer:	*We will be discussing our new product entry, so we must ensure that what is said at our meeting will not be overhead by anyone else in the hotel.*
Salesperson:	*Then absolute privacy is a must. Let me tell you about our secluded wing; it will provide the privacy and security you need. Not only is the meeting room soundproofed, but there is only one entry or exit to the wing. Consequently, no other guests will be wandering through the hallway on their way to another part of the hotel. Furthermore, this meeting area is housed away from the main building. How does that sound to you?*
Buyer:	*Sounds like that will work.*
Salesperson:	*Great! What other attribute is important to you?*

Presentation Techniques

A list of "do's" and "don'ts" to keep in mind when giving a presentation are included here.

Presentation Tips and Techniques

Do's	Don'ts
be excited	interrupt
rephrase	use slang
summarize	be late
be attentive	assume
document	generalize
be assertive	argue
smile	talk more than customer
listen	disparage
trial close	wing it
plan	procrastinate
homework	frown
be enthusiastic	take coffee breaks
have lunch with buyers	wait to get help
follow up	complain
promise a benefit	be intimidated
render a service	look unhappy
ask for leads	be impatient
ask for the order	don't assume the customer will just buy when ready

Verbal Tips

Just as there are good delivery techniques that should be practiced, there are also some words that should be used and others that should be avoided in the sales presentation. Select words that are effective and have strength or a descriptive quality. Avoid words like "nice, pretty, good, and cool." These words lack strength and diminish the quality of your product. At the same time, avoid sales terms such as "A great deal!" "No problem!" and "I guarantee you will."

Furthermore, because some prospects are uncomfortable making decisions, you should select words that allow these prospects to mentally reduce their accountability for the decision. The following list provides good words that you should substitute for bad or "trigger" words (that might encourage the prospect to continue delaying the sales process):

Good Words	Bad Words
total investment (value)	price or cost
initial investment	down payment
agreement/paperwork	contract

(continues)

Good Words	Bad Words
own	buy
presentation	pitch
opportunity	problem
ok the paperwork	sign
approve the agreement	order

Communication Tools

Although the preceding techniques maintain the prospect's attention and improve understanding, they do not necessarily help the prospect remember what you have said. Remembering the facts of your presentation can be critical if the prospect will be conveying information to others who will be helping to make the decision or if the prospect is hearing numerous sales presentations before making a decision.

It can be very helpful to use visual communication tools to aid the prospect's memory of your presentation. For example, develop charts, pictures, illustrations, and brochures that can be left with the prospect to facilitate his or her memory. Utilize models, samples, gifts, product demonstrations (site visits), and letters of testimony from satisfied customers during your presentation. For greater drama, also consider using electronic media—slides, videos, computers, and overhead projections—that can have a strong visual impact on the prospect.

 ## Reason-to-Buy Exercise

You are now in the sales division for the Surfside Hotel, a prestigious, four-star, 672-room, Italian Renaissance-style hotel located in Palm Beach. Amenities of the hotel include a new spa and specialized spa equipment; six restaurants, including an award-winner; a golf course designed by Robert Trent Jones; three lounges; a large pool area; and extensive meeting facilities. The hotel property also includes a private beach. You are going to call on Ms. Jones, director of the American Marketing Association in Chicago. One of her duties is to head the site selection committee for the semi-annual AMA conferences. The sites are selected two to three years in advance. Currently, the AMA utilizes the Breakers Hotel in Palm Beach (down the street from the Surfside Hotel) for its conference every other year. The AMA conferences are usually well attended, attracting more than 300 people to the winter conference. These conferences require extensive meeting facilities for concurrent sessions, an exhibit hall, and a banquet hall. Your objective is to persuade Ms. Jones to book a winter conference with the Surfside Hotel, and possibly seek a long-term agreement for returning every two or three years.

Take ten minutes to develop the lists indicated below in preparation for a two-minute presentation to a co-participant in this exercise who will be role-playing Ms. Jones. Be prepared to use good communication skills, comfortable body language, and many reason-to-buy statements (a combination of owner benefit and product characteristic statements).

Benefits to AMA　　　　　　　　　　**Supporting Hotel**
Re: Ms. Jones　　　　　　　　　　　**Characteristic**

_____　　　　_____

_____　　　　_____

_____　　　　_____

_____　　　　_____

_____　　　　_____

_____　　　　_____

_____　　　　_____

Key Concepts

Chapter 7 discusses the delineation between product characteristics and owner benefits. It also describes the progression of owner benefits process (POB), and then wraps up with tips for improving oral communication. The highlights of this chapter include:

- Owner benefits define the benefit that the buyer will obtain by purchasing the salesperson's product. A product characteristic is a part or feature of the product.
- Reason-to-buy statements combine the owner benefit and the product characteristic that creates that benefit into one forceful, effective statement. Reason-to-buy statements should be used frequently.
- The progression of owner benefits process assists the salesperson in understanding how the one owner benefit created by the salesperson's product can lead to additional owner benefits. The goal of this process is to encourage the salesperson to recognize "higher order" benefits that the salesperson's products may generate.
- Effective oral presentations should be verbally descriptive, energetic, interesting, and address the prospect's needs. Facts should be supported by visual aids such as charts, pictures, illustrations, site visits, brochures, gifts, product demonstrations, and letters of testimony.

Endnotes

[1] Heiman, Stephen E., Diane Sanchez with Tad Tuleja (1998) *The New Strategic Selling*, New York: Warner Books, Inc.

[2] Marchetti, Michele (1996), "Talking Body Language," *Sales and Marketing Management* 148 (October), 46; Metcalf, Tom (1997), "Communicating Your Message: The Hidden Dimension," *Life Association* News, 92 (April), 18-21; Piscitelli, Paul (1997), "How to Wow an Audience," *Sales and Marketing Management* 149 (June), 63-68.

HANDLING OBJECTIONS

n important part of the sales interview involves uncovering objections. An objection is an expression of buyer concern. Experience shows that it is rather naive to expect that telling another person everything known about the situation will convince that person to logically accept the idea or program. Facts, in and of themselves, do not sell. People interpret facts in their own way, see what they want to see, and hear what they want to hear. The assumption that facts will sell assumes that people are logical and objective. People are, of course, more emotional and subjective. Therefore, it is extremely important to recognize the opportunities to clarify objections. Rather than argue for a point when an objection is raised, a salesperson can be more successful by listening, or probing, to find out why it is an objection. The worst objection is the one not heard—the one the prospect refuses to disclose. A salesperson cannot overcome an objection that is hidden.

Why Prospects Object

There are a number of reasons prospects may provide objections to your proposal or product. First, prospects will not buy a product they do not understand. It is possible that you have talked over the prospects' heads. You must probe throughout the sales interview to ensure the buyers understand and agree with what you are presenting. Get into the habit of routinely asking, "How does that sound to you?" as you progress through the sales presentation. Second, the prospects will object if they feel the product doesn't fit their needs. In this case, you have either failed to qualify the prospects or did not sufficiently establish the prospects' needs for your product. A third reason prospects will object is if the cost is too high. You should learn the prospects' financial limits and keep them in mind as you progress through the sales process. Fourth, the person to whom you have been presenting may not be the decision maker. It is critical in the preapproach or approach stages that you clearly identify the decision maker so that you do not waste your time speaking to the wrong person. Sometimes prospects object simply because they are looking for the best deal, in which case, you should have identified price as the primary criterion and been prepared to overcome this objection. Another reason for objecting may be that the buyers are just seeking to challenge the salesperson, or that the prospects are uncomfortable making a decision. Finally, prospects may object because they perceive the risk as too great. In the latter situation, you have simply not convinced the potential buyers of the value of the benefits.

Steps for Handling Objections

When you encounter an objection follow these steps.

1. Listen and observe to gain time so that you can effectively counter the objection.

2. Check for understanding. Rephrase the objection to verify that you understand it correctly, so you can narrow the objection down to a specific point.

3. Use a positive statement with the prospect. You don't have to agree with the prospect, but you can let the prospect know that you understand why that person feels as he or she does.

4. Empathize and relate. Say things like, "I can understand how you feel," "I'm glad you brought that up," "Others have felt the same way," or "If I were in your position, I'm sure I would have arrived at the same conclusion."

5. If appropriate, construct a conditional statement. If the objection is based on price, respond with "If I could show you how you can afford our services, then would you be interested?" If you get a negative response, continue probing. The prospect may have an undisclosed objection.

6. Convince the buyer by providing evidence. Offer "proof" to back up your statements. For example, you may want to provide copies of articles, company literature, letters from satisfied customers, or names of references.

7. Verify agreement. After you have responded to the objection, confirm that the prospect has accepted your response. You might ask, "Have I explained myself clearly?" "Before we go on, do you have any other questions about . . . " or "Does this satisfy your concern regarding . . ." If agreement does not exist, you will need to continue probing.

8. Ask for the action needed to progress the sale. This may mean asking for the order or getting the buyer to commit to some other specific step.

Taking "NO" for an Answer

You must know how to take "no" for an answer. Certain essential actions must be taken before trying to close the sale again.

    ◆ Probe for hidden objections. When the customer says "no," it is for a reason. It is your job to probe for the reason and try to overcome the objection it represents.

◆ Recreate a "yes" frame of reference. The customer who says "no" finds it harder to say "yes." You not only have to probe for objections, but you have to get the customer in a "yes" frame of mind before again attempting to close.

◆ Every time a customer says "no," he unsells himself to a certain extent. You have to rebuild the sale, at least to the point where it was before you try to close again.

Listening and Responding to Objections

In any sales position, you will routinely encounter objections from sales prospects. Some common objections you may hear include: "I'm not interested," "I'm too busy," "I can't afford it," "I have no need for it," "Come back after vacation," "My partner's out of town," "My business is different." When listening to objections, you have to constantly ask yourself two basic questions about each buyer you deal with:

◆ What does that person *mean* by what he or she says?
◆ What does that person *feel*?

By *listening* instead of just hearing, you may avoid the trap of answering false objections. When you hear an objection like one of the above before the buyer has even heard your presentation, it can kill the sale. The early objection is often a purely personal reaction based on the buyer's personality and immediate situation. He or she may be tired, lazy, ill, or indifferent.

Two of the quickest and simplest ways to handle objections are to:

◆ Anticipate objections. Most objections can be anticipated and certain objections arise more frequently than others. Develop a variety of answers to such objections. Furthermore, if you know that certain objections are common, incorporate them into your presentation selling points to explain why they are not valid. This type of planning means fewer objections will be raised.

◆ Ignore early objections and proceed with the interview, outlining buyer benefits. Many salespeople turn a deaf ear to objections such as "See me next trip." or "I've got enough."

Additional Hints

Some additional hints for responding to objections include:

1. Listen to the objections and do not interrupt the prospect. Be a good listener as well as a good talker. Interrupting the prospective buyer, in many cases, increases the intensity of the objection and antagonizes the prospect.

   However, do not hesitate to be firm if the prospect interprets your silence as an opportunity to seize control of the interview. Standing silently by, while the prospect belabors a point or proceeds from one objection to another, consumes valuable time and accomplishes little. You may even find the interview has completely stalled.

2. Have the right attitude toward objections. Consider an objection a request for additional information and, therefore, an indication of interest. Regard this request as a question and answer it accordingly.

3. If the answer to an objection involves a point that you will cover later in your presentation, or if you feel confident the strength and persuasion of your presentation will overcome the objection, postpone answering by saying, "That's a good question and I'll come to it in just a moment, but first let me show you this." Occasionally, when such an objection is raised and it is the first indication of real interest, it may be advisable to hold the prospective buyer's interest by answering the objection immediately and to change your presentation accordingly.

4. Never repeat the objection. In answering an objection such as, "You have the worst service in town," don't repeat with an amazed look, "I have the worst service in town?" Also, don't say, with the same amazed look, "What?" hoping to minimize or ridicule the objection. You are not going to shame the prospect into retracting confidence in his or her own opinion. In fact, it is more likely the prospect's conviction will be strengthened. If necessary, answer the objection, but do not emphasize its importance by repetition.

5. Make your answer clear and brief. Do not magnify the importance of any objection by talking about it too much.

6. Don't lose your temper and argue or contradict. You can win the argument but lose the sale. The "Yes, but" technique can often be used to answer objections. In substance, you say, "Yes, I agree with you up to a certain point" or "I understand how you feel, but there is something you may want to consider."

   In using the "Yes, but" technique, avoid paying lip service to the "yes" portion; you must agree with part of the objection. Assume a prospective buyer states, "I won't hold my meeting with you because I'm short on planning time."

   Wrong reply: "Yes, but your staff deserves something better."

7. Whenever you can, turn the objection to your own advantage by making your answer bring out a selling point. For example, agree with the prospect that a condition such as shortage of planning time exists and then go on to explain how letting your staff handle the meeting will help solve the problem.

8. In handling an objection that involves dissatisfaction with your company's policies or disgruntlement due to a possible error, do not let the prospect influence you into condemning your company. Justify your company's position with dignity and make every effort to correct any errors. Your loyal stand will be respected far more than a pitiful "Don't blame me" attitude. To your

customers, you are the company, and you must assume direct responsibility for the proper execution of all company policies.

9. Finally, if you have been unsuccessful in getting the order, in spite of your efforts to overcome objections and close the sale, maintain your goodwill. You should try to leave the prospect with the idea that you are sorry not to have been able to help and that you will attempt to devise a better solution.

Techniques and Tools for Responding to Objections

There are many ways to handle objections. The most effective method will depend on the objection itself and the prospect's social style. You should be in command of many methods for handling objections so that you are never stymied. Here are just a few of the methods you may want to consider adding to your repertoire.

Price Method. Price is the most frequently mentioned objection. To handle this objection, gain a better understanding of the prospect's viewpoint by asking probing questions such as, "Too high in what respect, Mr. Jones?" or "Would you mind telling me why you think my price is too high?" These types of questions should elicit more information from the prospects which allows you to better counter this objection. You should focus on selling the value and quality of your product, and emphasize features that justify a price difference. You can provide evidence of value and quality by demonstrating the product, providing testimonial letters, showing test results, or presenting independent studies. Discuss your superior service or company reputation.

Direct Denial. Provide information and correct facts, and present evidence to support your statement. However, this method should be used with caution; no one likes to be told that he or she is wrong. Consequently, this method should be used only when the prospect has presented an objection containing misinformation that could be harmful to the reputation of your company. "I'm sorry, Mr. Smith, but our hotel is not closing. Indeed, as you can see here, our annual report indicates how well we have been doing."

Indirect Denial. Recognize the buyer's position, but supply information to support your response to the denial. "I can understand how you believed that our restaurant was the one that was linked to several cases of food poisoning, but that restaurant is actually down the street from ours. Here is the newspaper article about that incident."

Compensation Method. If the product has certain shortcomings that the buyer has pointed out, the salesperson can admit the shortcomings, but show how other advantages of the product/service outweigh the disadvantages. "Yes, our guest rooms are smaller than the competition, but no other property offers a private beach."

Translation Method. Turn an objection into a reason for buying. "Our hotel is further from the downtown area, but this should result in better attendance at your sessions." Or, "Yes, our hotel is smaller than those you have used in the past, but we will be able to give you more individual attention."

Feel-Felt-Found Method. The feel-felt-found method is one of the most effective techniques for handling objections. It acknowledges the prospect's objection as legitimate, but also provides reassurance that others were satisfied with your offering. "I can see how you feel, other clients felt the same way about our location, but they found our hotel could meet all their needs." When using this method for overcoming objections, evidence such as testimonial letters or the name and phone number of the third party should be provided to the prospect.

Boomerang Method. This method turns the objection into a reason for acting now. "I understand that price is an issue for you, but if you sign the contract now, I can guarantee you the lowest fare of the season."

Pass-up or Roll-over Method. If the prospect has presented you with an early, generalized objection, "I'm not interested in seeing any salespeople today," listen to the prospect, acknowledge that you heard, pause briefly, then go on with the presentation. Use this method sparingly. For example, a version of this was used by a salesperson who initially encountered a prospect who shouted out, "I don't want to see any more salespeople," as soon as the salesperson opened the door to the prospect's business. Rather than excusing herself immediately, the salesperson simply said, "It sounds like you've had a bad day. Why don't you tell me about it?" Thirty minutes later, the salesperson walked out with the sale.

Postpone Method. When the prospect raises an objection, the salesperson simply asks permission to address the objection later in the presentation. "I'll be covering that in just a few minutes. . . Is it alright with you if I continue from this point?"

The following are objection tools. With the exception of the final objection (where the buyer overcomes his or her own objection), these tools will not close the sale or overcome an objection. However, these tools will help you better understand why the buyer has not bought and gauge the buyer's level of commitment to the proposal. This, in turn, will help you determine your next step, be it the probing stage or a close.

The Process of Elimination Tool. Use the process of elimination tool for the buyer who will not tell you his reason for not buying. This method is different because it requires the salesperson to get the buyer into the habit of saying "no." The reasoning behind this is that in this process the "no" really means "yes." The method is demonstrated in this example:

Salesperson:	*"There must be something I've not conveyed very well. Can you tell me what it is? Is it the staff support?"*
Buyer:	*"No, that's good support."*
Salesperson:	*"The property itself?"*
Buyer:	*"No, it's a quality resort."*
Salesperson:	*"The room rate?"*
Buyer:	*"No, it's not that."*

Consequently, the buyer must admit everything is either okay or reveal the real objection to you.

The "I'll Think It Over" Tool. Another frequently heard objection is "I'll think it over." A salesperson was once overheard to respond to this objection by saying, "I guess that means no." —Obviously, there are much more effective responses!!! The "I'll think it over" objection is really a stall technique used by prospects. If you accept this stall hoping the prospect will buy at a later date, you will lose 95 percent of your prospects. A stall signals that you have not given your prospect a sufficient enough reason to buy now—after all, prospects buy when they recognize a strong positive benefit. Use the method demonstrated here to overcome this objection:

Buyer:	*"Sounds okay, but I need to think it over."*
Salesperson:	*"Good. You really shouldn't make a quick decision on an event of this size, and you wouldn't be thinking about us unless you really were interested."*
Buyer:	*"That's true, and I'll give it careful thought."*
Salesperson:	*"So you have all the facts. While you're considering, perhaps you could tell me it there is anything about our product that you aren't satisfied with. Is it the location?"*

Now you're back to the process of elimination. You can also handle a stall by asking questions that focus on benefits such as, "How would you benefit from our service?" "What do you find attractive about our service?" or "What advantage do you see in our offer?" When a stall objection is legitimate, set a new appointment to ensure your return.

Duke of Wellington Tool. This method for handling objections is the only close that physically involves the prospect. When properly used, the potential buyer will list all the reasons he or she should buy. Help as much as possible with reasons to buy, but let the buyer think of any reasons not to buy. Divide the paper so that reasons "why" (or "Pros") are on the left, and "why not" (or "Cons") are on the right.

Why   Why Not

The Final Objection Tool. With this tool your goal is to establish agreement that there is only one final reason for not buying, and that you have correctly identified that reason. Listen to the objection very carefully and to all the buyer has to say. Be sure you understand it. For example:

Salesperson:	*"Okay—I guess that's it—but let me be sure I understand your position. The reservation you have about our recreation facilities outweighs all the benefits we discussed for holding your meeting at our property?"*
Buyer:	*"That's right."*
Salesperson:	*"So then, nothing else, just the recreation facilities?"*

Buyer:	*"Everything else is agreeable. I just don't think there's enough recreation available for the 'free' time that will be scheduled during the meeting."*
Salesperson:	*"Would you mind going through that again so I can fully understand the importance of recreation during your conference?"*

As the prospect restates the concern, it might sound a bit irrelevant even to him- or herself, and the prospect will overcome his or her own objection. Or, the prospect maintains his or her conviction, but now you can deal with a genuine objection.

Caution: Only use the final objection tool if you know you can resolve the prospect's objection.

The Lost Sale Tool. After what appears to be the final decision, question why you failed. In short, ask the buyer why he or she did not buy from you. The lost sale close is a good way to identify a hidden final objection. For example:

Salesperson:	*"So I don't make the same mistake again, please tell me, what did I do wrong?"*
Buyer:	*"Okay, you failed to convince me that your room rate was the best deal I was going to be able to obtain."*
Salesperson:	*"I see, and that's your concern?"*

The buyer has stated a major objection. Instead of saying "no," the buyer is now saying "No, because..." and that leads back to the evaluation stage and an opportunity to satisfy the concern.

If the customer is not ready to buy, ask, "Is there some reason you're not ready to buy?" Don't push, but don't give up. Say something like, "May I send you some information and call you next week?"

 ## An Objection Response Exercise

For this exercise, write out a response to each objection given. Try to use a variety of response methods.

1. "I need to discuss your proposal with my partner."

_____

_____

_____

2. "The price you have quoted is way beyond my budget."

_____

_____

_____

3. "Let me think about it and I'll get back to you."

_____

_____

_____

4. "I know my account is not a big one. I am afraid that my company events will just get lost in the shuffle."

_____

_____

_____

5. "Your property doesn't have a swimming pool."

_____

_____

_____

6. "I understand your firm has run into legal difficulties and may not be open much longer."

_____

_____

_____

7. "I really don't like your proposal and would prefer to obtain bids from other companies."

_____

_____

_____

8. "I'm leery of holding the Christmas party at your restaurant, the last time I ate there the service was awful."

_____

_____

_____

9. "I'm not buying anything today."

_____

_____

_____

10. "I'm sorry, but we won't be using your hotel for our annual banquet this year. We've decided to try the new hotel on the waterfront."

_____

_____

_____

Key Concepts

Chapter 8 explores the process of recognizing and handling buyers' objections.

◆ Buyers will object if they don't understand the product, if they feel the product doesn't fit their needs, if the cost is too high, if they are not the decision maker, if they are looking for the best deal, or if they perceive the risk is too great.

- It is important for salespeople to listen and respond to objections. Most objections can be anticipated, but it is always important to understand and empathize with buyers' objections.
- Never argue with buyers over objections. Try to create a positive atmosphere during the sales call.
- The following techniques can be used to handle objections:
  - price method – use probing questions to determine value.
  - direct denial – present facts and evidence to support your statements.
  - indirect denial – recognize the objection, then provide evidence.
  - compensation method – give advantages that outweigh disadvantages.
  - translation method – turn an objection into a reason for buying.
  - feel-felt-found method – agree with the objection, but reassure prospect that other clients are still satisfied.
  - boomerang method – turn an objection into a reason for buying "now."
  - pass-up or roll-over method – address the objection later in the presentation.
  - process of elimination tool – determine a reason for the objection by exhausting a list of possibilities.
  - I'll think it over tool – avoid the stall tactic and determine the reason for not buying.
  - Duke of Wellington tool – have the buyer list the pros and cons.
  - final objection tool – narrow it down to one final objection and close.
  - lost sale tool – ask the buyer why he or she didn't choose your product.

GAINING COMMITMENT

aining commitment from a prospect—or closing the sale—is often an uncomfortable step for many salespeople. As was pointed out in an earlier chapter, in 70 percent of sales calls, the salesperson will not end by asking for the order. However, if you have used a consultative method of sales and have clearly identified and addressed your prospect's needs, closing should be an easier, more natural process. Consequently, asking for the sale should become more routine. This chapter discusses sales problems frequently encountered in the decision stage such as overselling, underselling, and not asking for the order. Next the chapter explains how to identify verbal and nonverbal buying signals, and then various methods of closing are presented. Finally, the chapter summarizes steps for obtaining agreement.

Common Mistakes in the Decision Stage

Most salespeople rate "closing the sale" as one of their toughest problems. It is not hard to imagine that the ease of closing is generally in direct ratio to the selling job that precedes it. If the owner benefits offered in your presentation have been acceptable to the prospect and the prospect believes the benefits will result from the use of your offering, gaining commitment from the prospect is relatively easy. However, some salespeople, not being sure of how and when to close the sale, will reach a point where the close would normally be indicated and talk themselves right back to where they started. They **oversell**. Then, there are salespeople who attempt to write the order before doing a complete selling job or who won't even attempt to gain commitment unless the buyer brings it up on his or her own. These people **undersell**. In fact, many *prospects* feel that the number one mistake salespeople make is *not asking for the order*. This section discusses these common errors.

Overselling. It is important to understand why overselling is detrimental to your presentation. Let's look at it from the prospects' viewpoint. If you have made a good presentation and the prospects are satisfied that the benefits offered will improve their situation, and are believable, any further presentation is overselling. Overselling can create, in the mind of the prospects, a feeling of disbelief as to the validity of the owner benefits. It can also result in the loss of favorable attention because excessive repetition of benefits and use of other motivation tools can lead to boredom or confusion, which, in turn, causes an unfavorable emotional reaction.

What are some of the basic reasons behind overselling? First, the salespeople just have not established two-way communication between themselves and the prospects. Second, the salespeople do not know where they stand in the sales process because of a lack of understanding. Third, there are always those salespeople who are fearful of closing for one reason or another. All these reasons are interrelated and can be traced to one underlying cause—*lack of knowledge*. Fear, itself, is founded in a lack of knowledge. As previously discussed, the intelligent use of the probing questions and good listening techniques will supply the necessary knowledge for salespeople to determine their position in the sales process. This contributes to the elimination of fear.

To summarize, don't talk a sale to death. *Let* customers buy.

When a buyer asks, "What colors can you use to decorate the banquet room?"
  Don't say, "We can do all colors—mauve, red, hunter green, teal, navy blue, etc."
  Do say, "What color would you like?"
When a buyer asks, "Do you typically have many children at your resort?"
  Don't say, "During certain times of the year we have a fair number of children, usually during summer school vacation and school breaks. We do, however, have the ability to limit the number of children within certain areas of our resort. We can be very flexible in our control of guest rooms, and we will work to serve you if you give us a preference at least 10 days in advance."
  Do say, "So that I can better serve you, why is that important to you?" Or, "It varies. To what extent will this affect your meeting?" Or, "It varies, but we can plan around your meeting needs."

Underselling. There is the case of a salesperson who would enter a prospect's business and immediately ask "Want to buy anything today?" Nearby workers would call out "No" and then the salesperson would turn and leave. This true story is an extreme example of underselling, but underselling in not an uncommon mistake. In the case of salespeople who habitually undersell or attempt to close too soon, their problem stems from many of the same reasons overselling occurs—the lack of knowledge of where they are in the sales process and/or how to establish two-way communication and gain understanding. In addition, there could be a lack of true *product knowledge*.

When salespeople try to close too soon, they fail to gain the prospect's interest and have not given the prospects an opportunity to evaluate the offering to their satisfaction. Sales that are made in this manner are made by chance. It should also be remembered that attempting to close too soon can create an emotional barrier that results in the loss of favorable attention. Without true product knowledge and the understanding of its correct use, salespeople may well be fearful of the close.

Chapter 7, demonstrated how product knowledge can be gained through an intensive study of the characteristics of your product, service, or plan, together with the owner benefits that result from the use of the offering. This knowledge is the essence of selling. Without it, closing is one of the salesperson's toughest challenges.

Not Asking for the Order. The third, and most serious problem, is not asking for the order. This could be the result of one of the following reasons or a combination of them.

- The salesperson is afraid he or she may get a "no" or may not be sure of how to ask.
- The salesperson does not know where he or she is in the sales process.
- The salesperson is unsure of the prospect's level of understanding.
- The salesperson has subconsciously endowed the prospect with the same degree of knowledge, experience, and background that the sales person possesses and, therefore, can see no reason why the prospect should be asked to buy.
- The salesperson lacks knowledge of effective closing techniques.

All of the reasons given in the situation of not asking for the order, and in the overselling and underselling situations, can be overcome through an understanding of the prospective buyers' viewpoint and the fundamentals and principles of sales techniques discussed in previous chapters. You can help your prospects make their decision to purchase easier by knowing the prospects' needs, planning and making your presentation from the prospects' point of view, measuring the prospects' understanding throughout the sales process, and using the closing techniques discussed in this chapter.

It is no secret to your prospects that you are there to sell products, services, or plans and to get a commitment—the prospects expect you to ask them to buy. Therefore, whether you do it directly or indirectly, *always ask for the order*.

Buying Signals

The secret to closing is knowing when to close. A good salesperson has to be able to read and interpret the various signals that come up in a presentation that indicate it is time to seek buyer commitment. Some signals are easily detected; these may include statements of objections, indications of disinterest, or admissions that the prospect would like to buy. Other signals are not quite as noticeable, but reading them correctly can result in a sale.

Many times people may want to do something, consider it desirable, and still hesitate, making excuses to put it off. For example, they might think to themselves, "It would be great to go to the beach today, but the crowds will be murder." Or, "I could use a new suit. Oh, I'll wait and look tomorrow." The same type of rationalization happens in a sales situation. The difference is that the customers express it to you. This type of customer rationalization means the prospects are just about convinced, but are hesitating and may talk themselves out of it. It is important to recognize this form of rationalization as a buying signal so you can capitalize on it immediately.

Buying signals can be physical or verbal. Physical signals consist of actions and movements. Unconscious nodding while talking; examining the product or handling it in a manner that indicates interest and/or satisfaction; the relaxing and softening of a facial expression; a relaxing of the body; leaning forward; and a thoughtful look are just some of the possible buying signals. The better you know your prospects, the easier it will be for you to "interpret" their body language and pick up the prospects' buying signals.

Verbal or spoken buying signals may be comments, suggestions, questions, even expressions of concerns. For example:

"That menu certainly looks good."
"It's certainly a novel idea."
"I don't like your room rate."
"I'd have to have guaranteed space by Friday."
"When do your off-season rates start?"
"How much space will it take?"
"Is that the best rate you can give me?"

When you see or hear potential verbal buying signals you must evaluate the statements by examining the actual words the buyers use. To be a buying signal, the statements or questions should be phrased with a certain amount of hesitancy and/or convey a feeling of indecision. The "rationalization" spoken of earlier will be showing through.

There are a lot of words that suggest the feeling of hesitancy that goes with a spoken buying signal. When the prospects use words or phrases like these, be alert for a buying signal. Here are some phrases that indicate indecision—a signal that the prospects are looking for help in making the decision.

I suppose	I don't think I should
maybe	I wish it were possible
perhaps	if I thought
it seems	I probably should
I wish I knew	I might

The tone of voice is very important in recognizing verbal buying signals. So, when you're looking for buying signal clues, evaluate the tone of the customer's voice as well as the actual words and phrases. The voice may indicate that the customer is hesitating, but still interested.

Besides evaluating how the statements were made, you must also consider where you are in the presentation. For example, if the prospects were to bring up the question of price *before* you've explained "why" the product will benefit them, it can be a brush-off or an indication of lack of interest in listening. However, the same question about price can be a buying signal if the prospects ask about the price *after* a show of interest or during an attempt to close on a summary of benefits.

Overall, you can pick up buying signals by maintaining a constant awareness of (1) what the prospect is saying, (2) how he or she is saying it, (3) what the prospect is doing, and (4) when the buying signal comes up. *When you detect a buying signal, there's only one thing to do—stop selling and gain commitment immediately.*

Salesperson Closing Behavior

To successfully obtain commitment, you must have a positive attitude that conveys confidence and enthusiasm. You must let the prospects set the pace because some customers absorb information very slowly while others absorb information very quickly. Control should not be an issue because you are trying to create a "win-win" relationship. You should be assertive, not aggressive. Aggressive salespeople ask few questions to determine the prospects' needs because they assume they know what the prospects want and they keep the prospects' participation down to a minimum. Submissive salespeople, however, socialize, but do not probe for the customers' needs; they just assume customers will buy when ready. In contrast, assertive salespeople are self-confident and positive. They probe for the needs of prospects, ask a lot of questions, encourage customer participation, and properly address objections—so the close is automatic.

Trial Closes

Sometimes salespeople are not sure where their prospects are in the buying process. Or, salespeople may have seen or heard something that they believe a buying signal, but are not certain. In these circumstances, salespeople can use a trial close. Trial closes are designed to provide information as to where you and the prospect are in the sales process. If you get a positive or favorable response to a trial close, you can move forward to the close. If you obtain a negative or unfavorable response, you can probe to identify concerns. Some trial closes that you may want to try include:

"In your opinion, do you feel that our product/service could be of benefit to your company?"

"What do I have to do to earn the right to do business with you?"

"Do you have any questions?"

"Do you have any other concerns?"

"Based on what you've seen, can you think of any other solution that would be better?"

"Do you like what I've shown you?"

"Do you feel this would help you solve that problem?"

Gaining Commitment

Buying is an active process that requires the prospects to make a decision. To the prospects, that's a very important step because the moment the prospects decide to buy, they become accountable! That could be very threatening, especially if the prospects are under pressure to perform, as are most buyers. Consequently, very few prospects will be quick to indicate their readiness to buy. Even when they are ready to buy, they may hesitate to make the decision because the normal force of inertia makes it easier for them to do nothing than to do something. That is why salespeople rely on closing methods to help gain commitment. If the prospects are ready to buy, you are actually helping the prospects to make up their mind. If the prospects have a reservation, you are better off knowing about it, so that it can be addressed.

Once the reservation has been identified and resolved, you should try to close again. In fact, you should be prepared to ask for the sale more than once from each prospect. Each time you should do it in a different way, so that the prospects do not get the impression that they are being pressured.

There are a number of closing methods you can use. Naturally, there is not one best method, so you should start by using the one you know best and as the situation changes, use others until the sale is closed. However, it is important that you become comfortable using a variety of closes so you can vary them according to the prospect's social style.

What follows is only a partial list of the more popular closing techniques that are available. You need to find those with which you are most comfortable, but also identify those that will work with different social styles.

Direct Close—Ask for It. Simply come straight out and ask for the decision.
Salesperson to Buyer:

> *"Can I have your okay on this booking agreement?"*

OR

> *"Can I block 100 rooms for your association members?"*

The Half-Nelson Close. To use the half-nelson successfully, complete product or service knowledge is essential. This can be used as a follow-up to a prospect's question or statement about your product, service, or plan. Simply stated—"Will you buy if it meets these requirements?" For example:

Buyer:	*"I don't think you have room for the meeting space we require."*
Salesperson:	*"If I can show how the hotel can accommodate your needs, will you book the meeting with me?"*
Buyer:	*"Can I get this room rate at the end of this month?"*
Salesperson:	*"If you can, will you sign the letter of agreement today?"*

Assumption Close. In an assumption close, you assume the buyer is accepting what you are offering.
Salesperson to Buyer:

> *"I believe we have most of the details worked out. I'll deliver the letter of agreement to your office on Monday for your okay."*

OR

> *"Will Thursday be a good day to approve the menus for the meal functions?"*

The Alternative Close (Either/Or Close). It often helps get the prospect's agreement by asking which is the most acceptable option. You are actually asking—"Will you buy it or will you buy it?" Either answer ensures a positive commitment.

Menu:	Chicken or beef?
Guaranteed Rooms:	35 or 40?

Loss Close (Standing Room Only). The loss close stimulates the buyer to capitalize on an opportunity that may not be available in the future.

Sales Representative to Buyer:

"This special rate ends Friday. If you don't book your event by then, you and your company will miss an opportunity to save money. Why don't we get the paperwork for your event completed now?"

Opinion Close. An opinion close overcomes the prospect's hesitancy by reinforcing his or her interest with an authoritative opinion from the salesperson or someone whose judgment the prospect trusts or respects.

Salesperson to Buyer:

"I believe that the way our meeting rooms are situated will provide you the maximum session participation while smoothing traffic flow . . . can I book your event for May 21st?"

OR

"George Mills, association director of the Life Insurance Marketing Research Association, said that our hotel site always attracts the most members to the annual meeting. Do you think 130 rooms will be enough for your group?"

Story Close. Most people do not like to be the first to buy a new product, implement a change or do something new. It is a natural reaction to fear the unknown or reject what is not understood. When salespeople have a new product to sell or a new concept to suggest to a prospect, they should tell the prospect about another customer who had difficulty in deciding whether to buy or not and, after the customer did, found that the decision had been the right one. Tell your prospect about the results that were obtained.

Salesman to Buyer:

"Several key customers have used the layout with one large meeting room and three smaller breakout rooms to the right and left of the main room. This configuration worked very well for them. Can I put you down for the same thing?"

Concession Close. The concession close involves using incentives to induce the buyer to accept your offer.

Salesperson to Buyer:

"If I guarantee this rate, will you agree to the rest of the terms?"

OR

If I provide the meeting space free of charge, do we have a deal?

Sum-Up Close. The sum-up is an excellent close to use. You simply enumerate the benefits (not product characteristics) that you and the prospect have agreed upon. Then, you shift to an assumptive close. Notice, in this example, the salesperson emphasizes benefits when the prospective buyer is already mentally weighing cost against gain. In effect, the salesperson brings out the important factors that will help the prospect make a sound decision. By using statements that seek the prospect's agreement, the salesperson makes sure the prospect understands the benefits of the offering, and the salesperson verifies where he or she stands in the sales process. The statements are also used to focus greater attention on those benefits of principal importance to the prospect.

Salesperson to Religious Association Director:	*"So we have agreed, Mr. Green, that your members can save money because of our low rates and complimentary breakfast."*
Buyer nods in agreement.	
Salesperson :	*"We have also agreed that the hotel's proximity to the convention center will provide the greatest convenience to your members."*
Buyer :	*"Yes, that's right."*
Salesperson :	*"As we discussed, our hotel has a gym and a swimming pool that can provide your members with healthy activities when they are not at the convention center."*
Buyer :	*"No doubt about that."*
Salesperson :	*"Furthermore, we have agreed that our complimentary hospitality suite, based on your guarantee of 75 guest rooms, will provide the perfect meeting spot for your members."*
Buyer :	*"Yes, that's right."*
Salesperson :	*"Great! I can deliver the letter of agreement on Tuesday for your final approval."*

The Order Form Close (Helpful Tool). With the order form close, question and obtain the customer's commitment on the different stages of completing the order form.

Ask questions like:

> "Can I confirm your address?"
> "Can I confirm your phone number?"
> "Can I confirm this booking date?"
> "Will you okay this for me?"

When the order is submitted to the buyer for a signature, remember to ask for an okay or an approval—not a signature.

Relationship Close. After identifying the needs of the prospect through probing questions, you can say, "Based on what you have told me, I recommend you do _____, for the following reasons." Then, explain why the recommendation you are making is the best one for the prospect. You can end by saying, "Can we get started today?"

CLOSING (SUMMARY SHEET)

Purpose
Make it easier for the buyer to buy than to refuse.

Things to Watch For
Buying Signals:	physical	spoken

Things to Avoid
Overselling	Underselling	Not asking for the order

Principles of Closing
1. When you detect a buying signal, stop selling, and close fast. Use a trial close if you are unsure of where the prospect is in the decision process.
2. Always close once you've answered an objection.

General Closing Techniques
ask for it (direct close)	loss	sum-up
half-nelson	opinion	order form
assumption	story	relationship
either/or	concession	

A good closing could be your best opening.

TEN STEPS IN OBTAINING AGREEMENT (SUMMARY SHEET)

1. Figure out beforehand the needs of the person(s) to be influenced.
   a. Don't rely entirely on your own appraisal.
   b. Ask others.
2. Decide on a plan of attack.
   a. Timing? Mood? Enough time available?
   b. Consider the two to three most-likely objections and what you will do when they are raised.
3. Present idea.
4. Get prospect's reaction to your idea. For example, you could ask:
   "How does this idea strike you?"
   "What is your reaction to this approach?"
5. Listen to the prospect's reaction.
6. Don't accept the prospect's first objections. For example, you could ask:
   "In addition to that, isn't there some other reason why . . . ?"
7. Explore the problem. Draw the prospect out in conversation; get talking—and then listen.
   a. Open-ended questions.
   b. Directive questions.
   c. Reflection.
8. Clarify the differences. "Let's see, we agree on these points, but not on this one, is that correct?"
9. Integrate; offer alternatives; check to see if objections have been answered.
10. Tie it up. Arrange some starting date or at least the next step.

 Buying Signals and Closing Exercise

Look over the following situations:

- Circle the genuine buying signals.
- Prepare a closing statement to match each situation.

1. "Your proposal sounds good, but we already have three hotels with which we usually do business."

2. "Your proposal looks good all right, but I'd better think it over when I have more time."

3. "I haven't seen this idea presented before."

4. "I understand the major points of your proposal."

5. "I only wish our meeting schedule were flexible enough to consider other properties."

6. "I'll go along with you on the banquet theme idea, but I don't think the other idea is that great."

7. "Man, you're out of it . . . look, I have to be very price conscious and you've got the guts to ask me to book my event at your property without any deal . . . get out of here!"

What to Do if the Buyer Says "Yes"

If the buyers respond favorably to your close, then confirm the buyers' choice by making them feel secure about the decision to buy. Obtain the signature or other form of approval that you need to process the sale. Do not appear overly eager or excited when the customers are about to sign. Thank the customers. And, finally, follow through on the sale. Make sure the buyers get everything you promised.

What to Do if the Buyer Says "No"

Sometimes, despite your best attempt, you are not going to close the sale, even though you have previously qualified the prospect. In reality, the majority of prospects do not buy, so you must be prepared to hear "No!" When you do get a "no," examine possible reasons for failure. Did you reflect a poor or negative attitude? Did you lack confidence? Did you not explain the benefits well? Was it simply the wrong time or place for the presentation? Did you talk too much and not listen?

If you recognize that you are having difficulty making sales, perform a detailed self-evaluation using the checklist we have provided on the following pages. By conducting this self-evaluation after every failed sales call, you should be able to identify your problem areas and then you can work to correct them.

My Failed Presentation Self-Evaluation Checklist

Yes	No	Questions	How Could I Improve On My Next Call?

My Preparation

_____ _____ Did I carefully review beforehand all the material I had gathered on this prospect's operation or circumstances?   _____

_____ _____ Did I anticipate trouble by figuring out which objections were likely to be raised and planning the most effective ways to answer them?   _____

_____ _____ Did I pick out a few sales aids to use and decide when to use them?   _____

_____ _____ Did I preplan the most effective way to demonstrate my product or service?   _____

_____ _____ Did I select my approach carefully enough beforehand?   _____

_____ _____ Did I preplan several trial closes and figure out when to use them?   _____

_____ _____ Did I prepare for this interview as carefully as possible, without skipping a single step to save time or effort?   _____

My Approach

_____ _____ Was I awkward in approaching and greeting the prospect?   _____

_____ _____ Did I greet him or her pleasantly and go right into my planned approach?   _____

_____ _____ Was I inwardly proud of being a salesperson and of my company and product?   _____

_____ _____ Was I businesslike in my approach?   _____

_____ _____ Did I feel nervous and timid?   _____

_____ _____ Did my opening remarks arouse interest and make the prospect want to give me some of his or her time?   _____

_____ _____ Did I find that the elements of the sale were really there: the need, the ability, and the authority to buy?   _____

Creating and Holding Interest

_____ _____ Did I quickly arouse and hold my prospect's attention and interest?   _____

(continues)

My Failed Presentation Self-Evaluation Checklist *(continued)*

Yes	No	Questions	How Could I Improve On My Next Call?
_____	_____	Did I encourage the prospect to talk and then did I listen attentively?	_____
_____	_____	Did I create the impression that I was sincerely trying to help the prospect?	_____
_____	_____	Did I get the prospect to ask questions? Did I answer them to his or her satisfaction?	_____

Raising Interest and Securing Conviction

Yes	No	Questions	
_____	_____	Did I make my whole presentation, or at least all the key points?	_____
_____	_____	Did I refuse to let questions, objections, or interruptions throw me off the track?	_____
_____	_____	Did my product or service really meet the prospect's needs and offer true benefits?	_____
_____	_____	Did I cover all the benefits of my product?	_____
_____	_____	Did I establish the need for at least two of those benefits?	_____
_____	_____	Were the benefits I stressed the ones of greatest interest to the prospect?	_____
_____	_____	Did I bring out the strong points of my proposal?	_____
_____	_____	Was I enthusiastic about the benefits?	_____
_____	_____	Was I convinced that the prospect would benefit from my proposal?	_____
_____	_____	Did I get point-by-point agreement on the value of the benefits?	_____
_____	_____	Did I prove the value of my proposal?	_____
_____	_____	Were my statements consistently positive and not negative?	_____
_____	_____	Did I win the prospect's confidence?	_____
_____	_____	Did I secure conviction that my product could fill his or her needs?	_____
_____	_____	Did I recognize buying signals and try to turn them into trial closes?	

My Failed Presentation Self-Evaluation Checklist *(continued)*

			How Could I Improve
Yes	No	Questions	On My Next Call?

My Demonstration

Yes	No	Questions	How Could I Improve On My Next Call?
____	____	Did I use all my sales aids effectively?	_____
____	____	Did I fumble or have trouble finding and using my sales-kit aids?	_____
____	____	Did I show all my samples or demonstrate my product /service to show its value?	_____
____	____	Did I show too many samples or sales aids and thus confuse the prospect in any way?	_____
____	____	Was my demonstration disjointed and thus unclear?	_____
____	____	Was I able to get the prospect to participate in my demonstration?	_____
____	____	Did the prospect fully understand all the points of my demonstration?	_____

Handling Objections

Yes	No	Questions	How Could I Improve On My Next Call?
____	____	Was I successful in getting the prospect to voice all of his or her objections?	_____
____	____	Was I able to restate those objections in the form of questions, and to handle them as questions that I was happy to answer?	_____
____	____	Was I able to get the prospect to explain the basis of these objections?	_____
____	____	Did I show any irritation with any objections, questions, or negative responses?	_____
____	____	Did any objections or questions rattle me and throw me off track?	_____
____	____	Was I able to turn objections into yes-building questions?	_____
____	____	Was I able to answer all questions effectively?	_____
____	____	Did I attempt to turn any objections into a trial close?	_____
____	____	Did I misrepresent my product or service in any way?	_____
____	____	Did the prospect raise any questions that I disregarded?	_____

(continues)

My Failed Presentation Self-Evaluation Checklist *(continued)*

Yes	No	Questions	How Could I Improve On My Next Call?

Handling Objections

Yes	No	Questions	
____	____	Was I well enough informed about my product and company policies to answer all questions?	_____
____	____	Did I avoid or fail to answer any valid objection?	_____
____	____	Did I lack conviction, pep, or enthusiasm in answering objections?	_____
____	____	Did I listen carefully to the prospect's answers, after restating objections or questions, and then handle them?	_____
____	____	Was I able to uncover all hidden objections?	_____
____	____	Did I uncover the real objection?	_____
____	____	Was I able to handle the prospect's complaint or objection promptly, properly, and to the prospect's satisfaction?	_____

My Close

Yes	No	Questions	
____	____	Did I use the trial closes I had prepared?	_____
____	____	Did I fail to recognize any buying signals or critical items to close during my presentation, prior to the summary?	_____
____	____	Did I secure the prospect's agreement to each point in my summary?	_____
____	____	Did I ever have the prospect ready to say yes and then lose the sale by overselling or simply talking too much?	_____
____	____	Did I inwardly give up the first time the prospect said, I'm not interested?"	_____
____	____	Could he or she have sensed my discouragement at any time?	_____
____	____	Did I uncover all the reasons the prospect would not buy?	_____
____	____	Did I ask for the order?	_____
____	____	Did I fail to suggest action now?	_____
____	____	Did I have only one closing argument?	_____

My Failed Presentation Self-Evaluation Checklist *(continued)*

Yes	No	Questions	How Could I Improve On My Next Call?

My Close

Yes	No	Questions	Improve
____	____	Did I keep a final, new, and strong reason to buy in reserve as a last resort?	_____
____	____	Did I know when and how to close?	_____
____	____	Did I let the prospect sell me on the fact that he or she was not interested or ready to buy now?	_____

My Personal Attitudes, Appearance, and Manner

Yes	No	Questions	Improve
____	____	Did I have a proper, positive, will-to-win attitude throughout?	_____
____	____	Was I confident and cheerful?	_____
____	____	Was my personal appearance satisfactory— was I dressed appropriately and well groomed?	_____
____	____	In general, did I feel, look, and act in a professional and businesslike manner?	
____	____	Was I proud and enthusiastic about my company and product or service?	_____
____	____	Did the prospect seem annoyed at some mannerism of mine?	_____
____	____	Did I knock a competitor?	_____
____	____	Did we get into an argument?	
____	____	Did I talk too rapidly or too much?	
____	____	Was I awkward and unsure of myself at any stage of the interview?	_____
____	____	Did I willingly discuss every important point the prospect mentioned?	_____
____	____	Did I talk at the prospect's level in terms the prospect understood?	_____
____	____	Did I avoid looking the prospect in the eye or fail to smile often?	_____
____	____	Did I use too many "I"s and not enough "you"s?	_____
____	____	Did I leave the interview pleasantly?	_____
____	____	Will I be welcome there on a callback?	_____

Key Concepts

Chapter 9 focuses on gaining commitment and closing the sale. In particular, three common problems or mistakes encountered by salespeople in the decision stage are discussed:

1. overselling – continuing to work on gaining commitment after the buyer believes the product will fulfill his/her needs.

2. underselling – attempting to close a sales before gaining commitment from the buyer.

3. not asking for the order – the salesperson does not properly read the buyer and does not know when to "close the sale."

Salespeople are less likely to make these three mistakes if they familiarize themselves with some of the common buying signals. Some of the easier signals to detect are:

- buyer making statements of objections
- indications of interest
- admissions of a desire to buy
- rationalizing

Buying signals can be physical or verbal in nature. Some physical signals include:

- nodding while talking
- examining the product or specifications and indicating interest
- a relaxed facial expression
- relaxing one's body
- leaning forward and/or offering a thoughtful look

Verbal buying signals may be comments, suggestions, or questions that demonstrate a genuine interest in the product by discussing details or using positive language. If a salesperson suspects the buyer is ready to purchase, but is not sure, the salesperson can use a series of trial closes to test the buyer's readiness. Once the salesperson feels he or she has gained commitment, the following closing techniques can be used:

- Direct close – just asking for the sale
- Half-Nelson close – ask "If I do this, will you sign a contract?"
- Assumption close – assume buyer is accepting what you are offering
- Alternative close (either/or) – get the buyer to make choices
- Loss close (standing room only) – let buyer know he or she needs to make a quick decision or the product may not be available at a later date

- Opinion close – reinforce the buyer's interest with a strong opinion from a salesperson or third party
- Story close – give an example of other buyers who made selection and were happy
- Concession close – get the sale in return for giving in to a buyer's demand
- Sum-up close – summarize agreed upon benefits and then assume the sale
- The order form close – fill out the order form as you discuss specific issues
- Relationship close – provide a solution based on buyer's stated concerns

POST-SALE FOLLOW-UP

I t is important to establish some kind of mechanism for obtaining information on the overall effect after an idea, program, or service has been accepted. "Follow-up" provides the opportunity to get more feedback on how people feel about the usefulness of the idea or service that was suggested or presented. It also helps to check customers' reactions about results accomplished when compared to their expectations. This chapter first discusses the meaning of follow-up. Next, suggestions are provided for following up with buyers and extending the relationship; these ideas are differentiated based on the four customers' social styles (amiable, analytical, expressive, driver as discussed in Chapter 3.)

Follow-up

Follow-up means doing what you have promised to do. Although salesperson follow-up has routinely been listed as one of the top selling traits most valued by customers, it is the one behavior in which salespeople exhibit the weakest performance.[1] If you tell a client you will do something—mail a brochure, supply needed data, etc.—be certain that you do exactly what you said you would do by the time promised. If an event occurs that legitimately prevents a timely follow-up, telephone your client and let him or her know you have not forgotten and you will follow up as soon as possible.

After you have made the sale, check back with the customer, and verify that everything is satisfactory. Do not let months pass before you contact the customer again. If the customer has booked an event with your hospitality organization, follow up within two days after the event to ensure that things went as planned. Your follow-up efforts can make all the difference in whether you will be able to obtain repeat business from this customer.

Follow-up Suggestions to Extend the Relationship

Just as you must adapt to each prospect's social style to make the sale, you must also adjust your follow-up and efforts to extend the relationship in the same manner. What works for one social style will not be as effective for another. The following paragraphs, discuss the most appropriate methods for following up and developing a stronger relationship with each social style category.

Amiable Customer. Do not remind amiable customers of details, even if important; identify one of the amiables' assistants who is detailed-oriented and get the amiables' permission to work with the assistant on the "mechanical aspect" of follow-up. Do not make the mistake of asking the amiables if they understand things, simply convey your assumption that amiables do. If the amiables wish for clarification, they will seek it; amiables tend to be "thin-skinned" and like to feel intellectually superior.

Clip articles related to the amiables' interests or your proposals, especially from publications dealing with the world of ideas, for example, *Successful Meetings*, and send them with a cover note soliciting their reactions. Appeal to the amiables' intellectualism by arranging for the amiable to speak before a prestigious group or by arranging for a summary of the amiables' views to be published in a journal. Invite the amiable to participate in social groups designed around intellectual pursuits (class group, bridge club, MENSA, economics discussion club, etc.), and feature them, if possible, in special roles having visibility.

Finally, cast the amiable customers in the role of your teacher or problem solver. For example, you could arrange a small follow-up meeting at which the amiables can brief your assistant, staff, or others. In other words, don't call the customers about your program per se; translate the call into a "problem that I need your help in solving—it's something I do not understand."

Analytical Customer. Analytical customers appreciate structure—ideas that are translated into specific sequences and steps. Analyticals do not like to deal with concepts or thoughts that are general, so you should follow up using a systematic approach. Analyticals' love of structure, and the sense of security it provides, will cause them to appreciate sales presentations and letters that are defined or explained in discrete phases or stages. That is, follow up your initial conversations with analyticals by discussing "Phase I" or "Step 1" of your proposal. In correspondence, use the same format. When you write analyticals a letter or memo, do not refer to having "several ideas." Instead, outline the program, refer to specific points, number them, and use subheadings (such as Phase II, Section I, Point Three). Similarly, analyticals love flowcharts, diagrams, and varying representations of the same data. Analyticals regard this as evidence of thoroughness, not repetition.

You should document everything. Analytical customers are very impressed by facts and prefer to have timetables to follow. It is also a good idea to accompany your memos with schedules and follow-up dates. Always keep analyticals appraised of what is happening with their company's program, meeting, etc. by providing both oral and written summaries on a routine basis (weekly or monthly). Since analyticals are basically cautious and somewhat insecure, they like to "go over" things and review them.

Many analyticals tend to nitpick concerning form; frequently, they seem to make buying decisions on the basis of quality packaging—appearance, form, etc. Analyticals evaluate things on the basis of whether they seem "professionally done." Therefore, try to be more formal in your approach and communication, even if it seems somewhat stilted.

Analyticals may be somewhat status-oriented. Analyticals enjoy having conferences and luncheon meetings in clubs. The atmosphere of a venue like the Harvard Club or the Sales Executives Club helps analyticals relate to tradition. These places are predictable to analyticals and help them feel secure and relaxed. Analyticals are also concerned about precedents, other users, testimonials, and user data. Unlike amiables who derive satisfaction from being first—a pioneer—analyticals like to be modern but tested, "Let a few others get the bugs out first." The analyticals are impressed if those they respect use your products or services.

Analyticals approve of understated appearances; they are conservatively inclined. When people dress flamboyantly, analyticals tend to be mistrustful of them. Analyticals like solid colors and stripes, and may have aversions to checks and free-form designs.

Expressive Customer. Expressive customers enjoy personalized relationships and do not "compartmentalize" their life. In other words, expressives do business with people they like. Expressives have a strong potential need to have each significant business contact be a friend as well as an outstanding, trustworthy professional. Becoming a friend to expressive customers is very important. Remember that expressives like dealing on a first-name basis. In addition, sincere interest in their family will be appreciated. For example, you should learn the names of expressives' spouse and children.

Be informal. Expressives like talking on the phone and frequency of contact is important. If there are long lapses between your calls or visits, expressives will feel you only want their business and are not really interested in them—this bothers expressives. When corresponding with expressives, one should convey warmth—and a light, personal touch. Also, recognize that the expressives do not mind being contacted evenings or weekends about business as long as you have established a good relationship with them.

Expressives like to go places with flair, such as restaurants that are international or unique in some way. For example, most expressives would not think it inappropriate to solidify the sales contract or implementation steps while sitting shoeless on the floor of a Japanese restaurant. Furthermore, expressives tend to be socially oriented. Therefore, invitations to sporting events, special parties, and other social events will be construed as loyal and meaningful actions on your part, especially when the events involve guests whose opinions they value.

Expressives like to know personal "tidbits" about competitors, others in their own organization, etc. Such conversation makes expressives feel "you're letting your hair down" and makes for a closer relationship. Expressives frequently have a sense of humor and enjoy humor in others; however, be aware that most expressives are concerned with "taste" and do not appreciate humor that is crude.

Finally, expressives place considerable emphasis on loyalty and sentiment. They tend to be sensitive and "thin-skinned," and no matter how secure they may seem in their positions, they do not feel secure. This insecurity exists because they tend to overreact to hints, nuances, political moves, possibilities, and pressures. Therefore, any efforts that are made resulting in their "looking good" to others who concern them politically will strengthen a long-term sales or client relationship. Any way you can credit them, their ideas, insight, decisions, etc., will count for a great deal.

Driver Customer. Driver customers prefer, and often insist on, brevity. Respect this. Drivers have a great sense of urgency. Consequently, as soon as you enter a room to have a discussion with drivers, it is wise to say, "I know you're extremely busy, so I'll be brief"—then get right to the point. Drivers appreciate candor and bluntness.

Go to the bottom line first and then work your way back. Drivers think this way—in terms of pragmatic outcomes—and they become tense and impatient in response to the "long windup."

Most drivers tend to interrupt. In dealing with drivers, encourage this. Drivers' questions are very astute. They are "testing" the realism of programs with these questions, so it becomes important for the salesperson to get used to interruptions and to encourage them.

Drivers are extremely competitive and combative. In communicating with drivers, identify their main competition, and frame your plans and programs as ways you can assist the drivers in disarming these people, or cutting them down to size. Many drivers consider themselves Robin Hoods without portfolios. They like to steal business from others and feel it is their moral obligation to do this.

Drivers tend to trust very few people; drivers are basically quite suspicious. Therefore, all follow-up plans will gain greater acceptance to the degree they feature built-in controls.

Since drivers are very impressed by nuts-and-bolts facts (percentage increase in bookings, restaurant ratings, or sales office performance), the sale or service must be reinforced by periodic written or verbal communications to them along these lines. It is perfectly appropriate to send drivers a single sheet from a computer printout with a red circle around the data you wish to highlight plus a one-line memo stating, "I thought you might be interested in this."

There is a "show me" quality in the makeup of most drivers; they are more impressed by actions than words. This trait can be an advantage to the experienced salesperson. If the salesperson positions new services or programs not as separate entities, but as vehicles to prove strategic points, the salesperson will enlist greater driver interest and curiosity.

Drivers like to roll up their sleeves and get their hands dirty. Visits with drivers should not be restricted to the "front office." If you ask drivers to take you into their operations—in order to meet the people, see the real problems, ask questions, and get the "nitty-gritty"—drivers will respect you as more the pragmatic and dedicated type that they see themselves.

Drivers are impatient and distractable. They often like working on several projects simultaneously and, therefore, receive many telephone calls and visitors at one time. Not surprisingly, they like this frenetic atmosphere. Drivers are often seen as crisis managers who like the excitement of many specific contests or challenges. Some salespeople have been upset with the drivers' lack of time for them, the interruptions, etc. However, the effective salesperson will learn to deal with the drivers on their terms, boil down the presentations to key points, and make faster closes. Indeed, drivers are always "testing" other people; if the salesperson has to do things "his or her" way, the salesperson will "lose points" with drivers.

Drivers are used to scheduling appointments on short lead time. It is possible to get an audience with them on 48 or 24 hours' notice. This is because drivers do not want to miss anything that could have a significant impact on their operations. However, you must approach the drivers on specific action points. Drivers will not schedule an appointment to review decisions already made.

Be prepared for cross-examination; drivers rarely take the time to be thoroughly prepared or informed on all aspects of a program or plan. Drivers believe in the 80 percent rule—by hitting highlights or key points they can decide correctly eighty percent of the time and the money they make by doing more deals in less time offsets the occasional miss. However, drivers don't want others to see this—particularly that the driver often tends to move too quickly—so drivers put others on the defensive. One of drivers' favorite techniques is to "spot-check" operations and "spot-check" people. Drivers will ask the salesperson four or five difficult and seemingly unrelated questions. The test is "on." Drivers care less about the information they receive than about the evidence of confidence, authority, and quick thinking on the part of the other person.

Key Concepts

Chapter 10 discusses the post-sale follow-up, or what steps the salesperson should take after the sale. Follow-up suggestions to extend the relationship are given for each of the four behavioral styles of customers:

- Amiable – avoid talking about details and let the buyer ask for clarification if needed. Let the amiable feel like he/she is helping solve problems.

- Analytical – likes structure and a systematic approach to things. Try to document everything and summarize your actions. Be conservative and reinforce the decision with testimonials and new information.

- Expressive – try to maintain a relationship and communicate on a personal level. Don't be too formal and make frequent calls and follow-ups. Show loyalty and appeal to his/her status-consciousness.

- Driver – use candor and be to the point. Focus on performance and the bottom-line, and demonstrate the practicality of your solution to his/her problem. Keep the driver informed and only make contact them if it is important.

Endnotes

[1] Graham, John R. (1995) "The 12 Deadly Sins," *Manager's Magazine* 70 (December), 12; Morgan, Jim (1997), "The Best Sales Reps Follow Up on Their Suggestions," *Purchasing* 123 (November 27), 65-68.

HOTEL CONTRACTS

I t is important for salespeople to consider components of the sales contract throughout the sales process. The ultimate goal of the salesperson is to reach a certain target revenue or profit for the entire account.

The purpose of this chapter is to identify each of the components of a standard contract, and to discuss some of the factors that need to be considered in negotiating the contract. All areas provide some latitude for negotiation, and there are tradeoffs that may need to be made during the negotiation phase of the sales process. Some hospitality facilities set minimum thresholds, but most properties operate within a particular range based on a number of variables. Some of the factors that will affect the negotiations are size of meeting, time of day/week/month/year, years until meeting, group history, potential for future business, and possible revenue from other sources. The areas that will be covered in this chapter include guest rooms, public space, food and beverage, cutoff dates, deposits, room rates, termination, and cancellation. Most hospitality chains have a standard letter of agreement that is adapted to meet the needs of the various types of meetings. It is difficult to cover all of the possible contingencies; therefore, the main objective of this chapter is to provide a template or checklist that can be used.

Guest Rooms

One of the first decisions a hotel must consider is how many rooms it is willing to commit to groups, and how far ahead it is willing to commit them. This decision will depend upon the individual hotel. Large conference hotels tend to commit a greater percentage of their rooms to groups. Also, they are willing to commit their rooms further in advance. Association meetings and conventions often require a large number of rooms from a hotel and, in some cases, need to use more than one hotel (citywide conventions). The lead time for these meetings can be five to six years, or more. Obviously, a hotel will also base this decision on the time of year and the days of the week. During peak seasons, most hotels will allocate more rooms to transient guests and corporate travelers who are willing to pay higher rates. Therefore, a smaller percentage of rooms will be allocated to groups and the hotel will be cautious about committing too far in advance. But the hotel should also consider the group's history and potential business in the future. Good clients can be given some concessions when it comes to these decisions.

The next step for the hotel is to decide the number of rooms in the room block and the mix of the various types of rooms. The salesperson should review the history of the meeting (say, for the last three years) to determine the likely attendance. This information can be obtained from the meeting planner or from a Convention and Visitors Bureau. It is important to realize that most meeting planners want to make sure they have an adequate number of rooms, and so they approach every meeting as if it will be the largest they have ever had. Consequently, meeting planners may overstate their needs, especially in the case of associations.

It should be remembered that associations often hold meetings to make money. The more people who attend, the more revenue they receive in the form of registration fees. As a result, the meeting planner's biggest fear is that people may decide not to attend because they cannot get a room at the conference hotel at the group rate. Some hotels use a practice referred to as "blind cutting," where the salesperson agrees on an inflated room block with the meeting planner, but then actually blocks a fewer number of rooms in the function book without the planner's knowledge. Hotels that use this practice are then responsible for finding attendees comparable space at another hotel in the event that they overbook the room block.

The types of rooms offered by the hotel may also vary. Most hotels have smoking and nonsmoking rooms, double beds and king size beds, concierge or business level, and suites. Some associations and SMERF groups (i.e., social, military, education, religious, and fraternal) have a large proportion of attendees who prefer double rooms because of the cost savings, while most corporate travelers prefer king size beds. In addition, it has been found that corporate travelers tend to have a higher incidence of smoking. The preferences of the various groups becomes important for hotels with limited availability of certain room types, and for conference hotels that rely on several groups at one time to fill their rooms. In some cases, hotels will have rooms with a view of an ocean, harbor, or downtown skyline that are limited as well.

The room rate is determined by the size of the room block, the history of the group, and the time of the meeting (such as peak versus off-peak period). In most cases, a hotel can quote definite room rates if the meeting is less than 12 to 18 months away. There is little chance that there will be any major changes in market conditions. However, when the meeting is more than 18 months away, it will be necessary to use one of the following methods:

- The current year's rate for this type of group, plus a negotiated increase to compensate for normal rate increases (this tends to be 4 to 6 per year); this approach will be best when the meeting is less than two or three years away.
- A negotiated percentage off the "rack rate" (i.e., the maximum rate charged by the property) for the year the meeting is scheduled; this approach can be applied to meetings that are as far away as 10 or more years, as long as the hotel uses the same philosophy to set its rack rate.
- The current year's rate for this type of group, plus an increase based on the region's Consumer Price Index or some other measure of the economic environment; this approach can be used for the intermediate to long-term range as well.

Once the method for determining the room rate is agreed upon, it is necessary to set a date when the rate will be finalized. This is usually done approximately one year in advance when many of the details regarding room blocks and meeting space are addressed. For meetings that are less than a year away, most of the details are finalized upon signing the contract.

It is important to discuss any other arrangements or terms that need to be considered. For instance, standard practice in conference hotels is to give complimentary rooms to meeting planners to be used at their discretion. The number of complimentary rooms is based on the total number of guest

1. Set dates for reviewing the group's history and adjusting the room block. The room block can be adjusted based on the most recent meetings held after the contract was signed.
2. Determine a formula that can be used for revising the group's room block. Use an average of the last three meetings, or weigh the most recent meetings higher. Take the arrival and departure patterns into account.
3. Set the final date for adjusting the room block without a penalty.
4. Determine the percentage of slippage the group is allowed at the final review date.
5. Develop a formula for determining damages in the event of slippage or cancellation (this formula can reduce the damages if any of the rooms are resold).

Figure 11-1 Guest Room Attrition Checklist

rooms used per night (usually one complimentary room for every 50 room nights). The complimentary rooms can be used for the association or corporate staff, executives, officers, or invited guests. Also, any provisions for free upgrades or hospitality suites should be documented in the contract.

The majority of most hotels' profits are generated from the guest room revenue. Therefore, it is necessary to protect this profit in the event of lower-than-expected attendance or cancellation. First, the cutoff date for holding the room block is established (normally 21 to 30 days before the meeting). After that date, the rooms are released to the general population and sold at the prevailing rate. Next, the contract should state the penalties for attrition based on a sliding scale. An allowable percentage for block reduction should be determined (for example, 10 to 20 percent), as well as a formula for calculating the financial damages. The formula could reduce the amount of damages based on the number of rooms resold—the group should only be responsible for lost profits (revenues minus expenses). Similarly, the contract should contain the terms for compensating the meeting planner in the event of overbooking. The hotel is normally required to "walk" the guests at the time of the meeting, but there may be additional damages based on the amount of room nights that the hotel cannot provide prior to the cutoff date. See Figure 11-1 for the Guest Room Attrition Checklist.

Meeting Space

When dealing with groups, salespeople must determine the amount of meeting or catering space that will be reserved for a specific group. Some hospitality firms try to keep things in proportion so that the public space allotted to any one group is a function of the number of guest rooms that they block or, in the case of restaurants, the number of meals guaranteed. For example, if a hotel allocates 500 rooms to groups and 200 rooms are blocked for a particular association, then the hotel is reluctant to reserve more than 40 percent of its meeting space for that group. It may be difficult to fill guest rooms at a later date with groups if there is not enough meeting space available. The only alternative would be to find groups that require meeting space, but not many guest rooms (weddings, reunions, etc.).

Another problem may arise if groups want to utilize public space that is shared with all guests, such as restaurants, pools, or bar areas. Some hotels will allow groups to reserve the pool area, and some restaurants will allow groups to reserve the lounge area for a reception or party, which will interfere with the needs of other guests. When this is done, the other guests should be notified well in advance so they can plan accordingly. Advance notification will minimize any ill will or dissatisfaction among the other guests. A similar issue may arise in hotels that hold conferences for multiple groups at one time. The public space must be allocated fairly between the groups with each of the group's needs being considered. For example, the hotel may only have one banquet hall that must be shared for luncheons and receptions.

The layout of meeting space can also be an important issue. First, it is necessary to keep track of the groups that will be meeting in the hotel or restaurant to ensure there are no conflicts. For example, there was a hotel in Texas that made the mistake of booking a meeting for a gun club at the same time a former president of the United States was staying in the hotel with his entourage of secret service agents. Needless to say, it was a harrowing experience for the agents to see rifles being carried and displayed around the hotel. Hospitality organizations should also avoid booking two companies that compete in industry or two groups with opposing views on political issues (e.g., gun control, abortion, gay rights). Second, the hospitality organization should understand the needs of the groups regarding meeting space. For example, an important business meeting should not be placed in a room next to a loud fashion show. Also, every effort should be made to keep a group's meeting space in close proximity to allow for good flow and movement between rooms.

Hospitality firms should consider all of the aforementioned factors when booking meetings and assigning space. This will eliminate customer dissatisfaction and help the firms build long-term relationships. Meeting planners are becoming more knowledgeable and they expect to be treated as professionals. It is not uncommon for meeting planners to ask to have meeting rooms listed by name in the contract. This will reduce the hotel's flexibility in booking other meetings, but it will ensure the meeting planners that they will have the required number of rooms with the necessary dimensions. An alternative would be to list minimum dimensions in the contract that could apply to various meeting rooms, allowing the hospitality firm some flexibility in making final assignments. Hospitality organizations should attempt to develop a specific policy regarding this issue.

The rates for meeting space vary widely between hospitality firms, and even within the same organization. Most firms will have rate sheets for their public space and meeting rooms, but they are willing to charge on a sliding scale related to the size of the group's guest room block or guaranteed meals. The rate for each room is based on the size (square footage) of the room and the length of time it will be committed to the group (24 hours or partial days). However, meeting planners are well aware that this is a common area for concessions. While there is an opportunity cost for having a meeting room sit idle, there are not any direct expenses associated with using a meeting room.

As mentioned earlier, if the guest rooms are filled, it is difficult to find other functions to utilize idle meeting space throughout the day. Also, it is important to remember that while associations are paying for meeting space, their attendees are paying for the guest rooms. Therefore, association meeting planners may agree to a higher room rate in return for complimentary meeting space. This is a win-win situation for both the hospitality firm and the association. Finally, it is common practice for hospitality organizations to begin to offer discounts and/or complimentary products or services when associations book a certain number of guest rooms (100 to 150 rooms) or guarantee a certain number of meals. The amount of discounts and complimentary items will differ by season—fewer concessions will be made during peak periods.

Food and Beverage

The food and beverage component of group meetings can be a difficult area to handle. Salespeople often lack experience or knowledge in this area and they can promise things in an attempt to secure a sale that may not be consistent with the normal operations in catering. Within a hotel, for example, the catering department is a profit center and its employees are evaluated based on their financial performance. What is best for the hotel may not be what is best for the sales department, the catering department, or the rooms division individually. Therefore, hotels should base rewards on team performance so that the various departments can work toward the same goals. If a salesperson's compensation is based on his or her ability to meet volume quotas, room rates and food and beverage rates may be reduced in an attempt to maximize volume.

In negotiating the food and beverage component of a contract, it is necessary to determine the menu and prices for the food functions, including refreshment breaks and receptions. Many large meetings prefer to have at least two entrees, one of which will satisfy vegetarians (for example, vegetable lasagna or fish). The rate depends on the hospitality firm's policy and the type of service. In some cases, groups opt for a buffet that reduces the labor costs and may provide more variety. Some hospitality firms have menus with fixed prices that are non-negotiable, while others are open to negotiation. In either case, it may be difficult to determine the exact price when the meeting is booked—it could be five or six years before the date of the meeting. Hospitality organizations can use the prevailing rate at the time of the meeting (or specified date) or assign a percentage discount that will be applied to the published rate at the time of the meeting (or specified date). Rates are often finalized at some point within one year of the event.

The prices for refreshment breaks and receptions depend upon the size of the group, the length of the function, and the type of food. There are general rules of thumb that can be followed for per-person and per-hour pricing based on the food and beverage offerings. Hospitality firms have price levels based on the types of hors d'oeuvres and beverages (top-shelf versus bar). Some firms will provide complimentary refreshment breaks if the group exceeds a minimum level of guest rooms and/or food and beverage expenditures. The other issue that needs to be addressed is gratuities. Many hospitality organizations have a required gratuity (17 to 20 percent) which is often dictated by the use of union employees that is added to the bill regardless of service quality. This needs to be included in the contract and made clear to buyers. In addition, some groups choose to cover all of the meals and gratuities for their members (for example, incentive trips), which should be written in the contract and conveyed to attendees.

One of the potential problem areas concerns association functions. There is an incentive on the part of association meeting planners to choose the lower-priced meals in an attempt to maximize their profit from the meeting. If the meal is included in the cost of registration, then the lower the price paid to the hospitality firm, the more that is left for the association. Unfortunately, attendees tend to blame the hospitality firm for serving "rubber chicken" or small portions, especially if the meal tickets are marked up and resold to the attendees. Therefore, hospitality salespeople should try to reason with prospective buyers and explain that it is a lose-lose situation. The hospitality company receives poor ratings and meeting attendees are not satisfied. Attendance at future meals and conferences may decrease, resulting in less money for the association and potential penalties.

The second step in the food and beverage contracts process is to assign the public space. This will depend on the size of the function and the type of setup. Larger functions are typically set up in rounds, while smaller functions have more flexibility for the setup. Hospitality organizations that host these types of functions generally have temporary barriers that can be used to convert a relatively large meeting space into smaller meeting spaces that offer a better fit for smaller groups. Once again, it is important to consider the types of groups that will simultaneously utilize the hospitality organization's facilities and assign space accordingly. Serious business functions should not be adjacent to motivational luncheons that tend to be rather loud. Other functions that tend to be loud are award receptions, weddings, reunions, senior proms, and college formals. Hospitality firms may be limited by the size of the food function, but every effort should be made to keep luncheons and receptions close to the group's other meeting rooms for easy transitions.

The last step is to determine the final date for meal guarantees and the penalties for cancellation or lower-than-expected attendance. Normally, the final number for meal guarantees is required within 24 to 72 hours of the function, depending upon the size of the group and the menu. Determination of the correct number is an easy task for corporate groups because attendance is mandatory, but attendance at association functions is voluntary. This, coupled with the fact that association meetings and conventions tend to be much larger, provide a real challenge for hospitality firms and meeting planners. Hospitality organizations could suggest that meeting planners hand out the tickets at the on-site registration booth after asking attendees if they plan on attending the function. Another option is for the meeting planner to charge attendees separately for the function rather than include it in the registration fee. Both of these methods should improve the accuracy of the meal guarantee.

The contract, however, must include a penalty clause for lower-than-expected attendance. Hospitality organizations should allow for a reasonable amount of "slippage" (such as, 5 to 10 percent), but prospective buyers should expect to pay a penalty when it is below the minimum number. The slippage percent will decrease as the size of the function increases. Also, buyers will be responsible for an agreed-upon penalty if the function is canceled. The penalty is usually calculated using a "sliding scale" based on the amount of notice given by the customer. The more notice given, the smaller the penalty. It is assumed that hospitality firms will be able to resell some of the space with adequate

1. Estimate the expected revenue from food and beverage functions for the meeting; adhere to minimum requirements.
2. Set a review date to determine a final figure for food and beverage revenue based on projected attendance; this date should coincide with the date for finalizing the room block.
3. Determine the allowable percentage of attrition (industry standard is 20 to 25 percent).
4. Develop a formula that can be used to calculate the damages (this formula can reduce the damages based on the amount of profit obtained by reselling the space).

Figure 11-2 Food and Beverage Attrition Checklist

notice. However, the contract can still hold customers liable for the liquidated damages based on differences between the realized profits and the projected profits that were guaranteed. Some hospitality firms hold customers liable for the entire amount that was guaranteed without adjusting for resold space, while technically, groups should only be responsible for lost profit.

Finally, the contract should also include information regarding better than expected attendance. That is, how many additional attendees can be accommodated and what price will be charged? There may be enough food to cover an additional 5 to 10 percent, but at some point, the hospitality firm does not have the food or space to accommodate the additional people. Again, association planners do not want to turn away interested members who may provide additional revenue or who may become disenchanted with the organization. Therefore, it is important to provide an accurate estimate of the projected attendance to avoid penalties, and accommodate members. See Figure 11-2 for the Food and Beverage Attrition Checklist.

Termination and Cancellation

There are situations under which the hotel or the group will need to terminate a contract and cancel a meeting without being liable for damages. The factors contributing to this situation are beyond the group's control. The following discussion includes the more of the more common reasons for canceling a meeting under these.

Acts of God are the most-cited reasons for legitimately canceling meetings. Neither hospitality organizations nor groups can predict hurricanes, floods, earthquakes, or snow storms, especially when booking meetings years in advance. Airlines aren't responsible for flights that are canceled due to weather because of the inherent risk to passenger safety. Therefore, meeting planners and hospitality companies can't expect attendees to risk their safety to attend a meeting if their means of transportation compromised. Similarly, meeting planners cannot hold hospitality firms liable for damages if the firm is the victim of one of these acts of God. For example, one of the authors was scheduled to go to a meeting in Myrtle Beach, North Carolina, a few weeks after Hurricane Hugo touched down on the coast. However, the first and second floors of the hotel incurred flood damage and the meeting had to be canceled (most meeting facilities are on the second and third floors of hotels).

Threats to health or safety can result in the termination of a contract. Acts of war are an obvious example of this situation. Since the early 1990s, not many meeting planners have been anxious to hold meetings in Yugoslavia. The safety of meeting attendees was in question amidst the fighting and civil unrest. Similarly, due to an epidemic or disease, a health risk is a legitimate reason for canceling a meeting. After people died from what was termed Legionnaire's Disease in a Philadelphia hotel, subsequent meetings were canceled until the safety of guests could be ensured.

Frustration of purpose refers to the reason why a group is holding a meeting. If the meeting surrounds a particular event and the event is canceled, the purpose for the meeting no longer exists. For example, many groups book rooms and rent meeting space in hotels during the Super Bowl. A few years back, the Super Bowl was to be held in Phoenix, Arizona. However, the state of Arizona refused to honor Martin Luther King Day and the NFL players and owners threatened to protest. If the problem had not been resolved and the Super Bowl had been moved or canceled, the groups would have been allowed to terminate their contracts without any penalties. The same would hold true for the cancellation of a parade or any other notable event. It is important that the customer makes sure that purpose of the meeting is known to both parties and is included in the contract.

Destruction of the means of performance refers to hospitality firms incurring damages that aren't acts of God. Meeting contracts can be terminated if a hospitality firm's facility has been damaged by something such as a fire or broken pipes. If buyers do not feel that the hospitality facility is offering the same service that was originally sold, they can attempt to terminate the contract. At the time the contract is signed, buyers should secure pictures of the facility and a clause should be added regarding this issue. It is very possible that meeting planners would not have scheduled a meeting years in advance had they known that the hospitality firm would be renovating the lobby or lounge. Also, something such as a labor strike may significantly affect the means of performance, as well as the safety of guests.

Key Concepts

Chapter 11 discusses the components of a standard hotel contract and some of the factors that are considered in negotiating contracts. The main areas of the contract are guest rooms, meeting space, and food and beverage.

Guest Rooms
- How many rooms you will commit to groups and how far ahead you will commit them?
- Determine the number of rooms in the room block and the mix of room types.
- Determine room rate based on the number of rooms, group history, and time of meeting. Set a date when the rate will be finalized.
- Discuss other arrangements like complimentary rooms and upgrades, and allowable slippage in the room block.

Meeting Space

- Determine amount of meeting or catering space based on the room block.
- Discuss utilization of other public space like the restaurants and pool areas.
- Determine the layout of the meeting space based on other meetings and the group's needs.
- Determine the rate for meeting space and discuss complimentary arrangements.
- Discuss the policy for meeting space rental in regard to cancellation or guest room slippage.

Food and Beverage

- Determine menu and prices for all food functions (such as, meals, breaks, and receptions).
- Prices for refreshment breaks and receptions should be based on the size of the group, the length of the function, and the type of food. Include the gratuities if necessary.
- Assign the public space based on the size of the function and the type of setup.
- Determine the final date for meal guarantees and the penalties for cancellation or slippage.

Typically, there are a few situations under which a contract can be terminated without the group incurring a penalty. The hotel contract should state those it will honor, but the following is a list of common reasons:

- acts of God
- threats to health or safety
- frustration of purpose
- destruction of the means of performance

SERVICING THE MEETING

alespeople are hired and trained to develop new business and fill group quotas for hotel rooms, catering facilities, and other hospitality spaces. In some cases, salespeople will continue to maintain accounts from the time the sales are made until after the meetings are held. However, in most full-service hotels, meeting planners are introduced to the convention services department or the catering manager to finalize the meeting plans. The reason for this transition is to allow the salespeople to return to their specialty, which is selling and generating revenue, and to place the buyer in the hands of people who specialize in servicing meetings. In this way, hospitality firms take advantage of the specialization of labor, enabling them to provide the highest quality service that is possible. In some hospitality organizations, there are not convention services departments, so the catering managers are in charge of servicing the meeting planners.

Making the Transition

The question becomes one of when to make the transition from the sales managers to the convention services managers. Large hospitality chains normally have executive meetings managers (EMMs) who handle smaller meetings (usually 20 or less people) with short lead times. Rather than make an awkward transition from sales to services, these hospitality companies find it better to allow the sales managers to handle the meetings from the beginning to the end. In fact, the EMM position is often used to train new sales managers in the nuances of the meetings business. It is also possible for smaller hospitality organizations to lack a large sales and services staff, making it necessary for the sales manager or the catering manager to handle all of the meeting duties.

In a situation where there are both salespeople and convention services staff, there are three points at which a transition can be made:

1. During the site inspection. In the process of conducting the site inspection, a sales manager could introduce the buyer to a convention services manager who will be in charge of their accounts. The services manager could be helpful in negotiating the terms of the contract, which would be useful for meetings with short lead times. However, during the site inspection may be a little premature and could actually confound the sales process.

2. Immediately after signing the contract. A popular time to make the transition is after the sales manager has made numerous sales calls and the contract negotiations have ended. The sales

manager can periodically contact the meeting planner leading up to the actual meeting, but the services manager will work on the details of the event. This allows the sales manager to allocate more time to obtaining additional business.

3. **One year before the meeting.** The last alternative is for the sales manager to continue to be the main contact person until one year before the meeting. This would coincide with the date used to finalize the meeting details for contracts that are signed well in advance of the actual meeting. The services manager could be helpful in finalizing the terms, especially for food and beverage and meeting space.

It is up to each hospitality firm to determine which transition alternative works best for its particular situation. Also, the transition alternative could vary based on the size of a meeting, the meeting planner's preference, and the lead time for the meeting.

The following sections will discuss the types of decisions that must be addressed in servicing a meeting. It should be noted that many of these areas are covered in the letter of agreement, but the details may not be listed. It is helpful to have some type of checklist covering these areas to make sure that there are no oversights.

Reservation Systems

One of the first areas of concern for servicing meetings is how attendees will make their room reservations. There are four possible methods depending upon the type of meeting and who will be responsible for making the payment.

- **Postal reply cards**. Postal reply cards are small cards included in meeting packets that are distributed to potential attendees. They are used mainly for association meetings and conventions. The cards should be clear and concise, and include arrival and departure dates, room rates, types of rooms, and any rules and deposit information. The reply cards can include the hospitality firm's direct number (possibly toll-free), which can be used to make the reservation as well.

- **Rooming lists**. Rooming lists are rosters of the attendees and their room assignments. The hotel merely needs to assign rooms to the people on the list. Rooming lists reduce the hotel's workload, and they are normally used for meetings with mandatory attendance (such as corporate meetings) or attendance that can be guaranteed (incentive meetings).

- **Toll-free numbers**. This method refers to the toll-free numbers used by hospitality firms. The problem with this method is that some hotels do not release the room block or provide pickup information to central reservations. Therefore, the reservation agents may find there are no vacancies when, in fact, there are available rooms being held by the hotel specifically for the group. This problem can be avoided by providing potential attendees with a specific code for the group. This method could be used for any of the meeting types.

◆ **City housing bureaus**. Most large cities have convention and visitors bureaus that operate a housing bureau for citywide conventions. A large convention may require room blocks at several hotels, and each hotel releases a certain number of rooms to the housing bureau at designated rates. In essence, the housing bureau serves as a central reservations service for meeting attendees.

It is fairly straightforward to determine what type of reservation system should be used in a given situation. The only real decision is between using central reservations or having a directed number for association meetings and smaller conventions. Most hospitality firms are choosing to use directed numbers in order to maintain more control. The types of rooms and the room rates are designated in the contract.

Function Room Assignments

The guest room control book will contain the room commitments by group, along with the availability and rates. Similarly, the **function book** contains the daily schedule for meeting rooms and public space. A separate page should be allotted for each day and one person should have the authority for making final assignments. There are various software packages that can be purchased by hospitality firms that automate the process of scheduling meeting space and food functions (for example, Delphi and Breeze). Tentative assignments are often made at the time the meeting is booked, but final assignments should be made approximately 60 days before the meeting.

As mentioned in the chapter on hotel contracts, several factors should be considered in making function room assignments. Primarily, the size of the room and seating capacity for the type of meeting room setup will affect the room assignment.

◆ **Auditorium or theater style**. Chairs are set up in rows facing the speaker, resembling a movie theater or school auditorium. This style can accommodate large groups. The general rule of thumb is to divide the room's square footage by six to obtain the number of people that can be accommodated. This allows for more people, but when people are crowded, there are bad sight lines, and it can be difficult to take notes.

◆ **Schoolroom style**. Chairs are set up in rows facing the speaker, but there is desk space like in a classroom. This style can be used for both small and large groups, but it takes up a lot of space. This style offers good sight lines and works well for presentations. The rule of thumb for schoolroom style is to divide the room's square footage by eight to obtain the total number that can be accommodated. You can typically seat two to three people per six-foot table or three to four people per eight-foot table.

◆ **Boardroom or conference style**. There are many variations of this style, of which the main purpose is to facilitate discussion. Although space and sight lines can be a problem, this style is often used for small groups. The rule of thumb is to divide the total square footage by ten to estimate room capacity. Some of the more common variations are the U-shape, the hollow square, and banquet style or "rounds." Banquet style is popular for food functions and usually eight to ten people per table can be seated depending on the size of the table.

Other factors that will affect the function room assignment are the type of event or presentation style, the room location with regard to traffic, and the room location with regard to adjacent meetings.

Food and Beverage

Several possible food and beverage components are associated with meetings. The three main types of food and beverage components for groups are meals, refreshment breaks, and receptions.

Types of Food Service

Hospitality firms can realize good revenues from catering for meetings. In conference hotels, banquet sales are often more than two times the sales from the hotel's restaurant(s). Banquets allow more price flexibility and the ability to serve a large number of customers in a short period of time. Food costs associated with banquets are lower because of the volume preparation and the fact that there are no large inventories. Attendance is guaranteed and food is purchased to meet the estimated attendance. Also, labor costs are lower and employee productivity is high. It is easy to staff banquets because of the guaranteed attendance and set time frame. Hospitality organizations often use part-time staff to whom they do not have to pay benefits; these firms only schedule as many workers as necessary. Finally, the beverage profits are high because costs can be easily controlled and there is a lot of price flexibility. People may not order drinks other than water in the restaurant, but meeting planners will order beverages such as tea or wine for all of the guests.

There are five basic types of food service to choose from for banquets or food functions. The best alternative will depend upon the number of people, the room setup, and the desired menu. Following is a brief description of each type.

- **Plate service**. This is the most common type of food service. The food is assembled in the kitchen and requires little skill on the part of service personnel. The plates are carried on a large tray from the kitchen and one is placed in front of each guest.
- **Pre-set service**. This type of service is good when time is an issue. One or more components of the meal are set on the table before the guests are let into the room (for example, first course, appetizer, and dessert). The food for this type of service is limited to what can set out for a while, and it may not be as attractive as other methods.

◆ **Buffet style**. This type of service can be very efficient for large groups. It requires less labor and more food items can be offered. People choose the items they want to eat, resulting in less waste.

◆ **Platter service**. This is a variation of plate service. Platters of food are placed on the table and guests are responsible for serving themselves and passing the food among themselves. It requires more work on the part of the guests, but less effort on behalf of the hotel.

◆ **European service**. This is the most labor intensive of all of service alternatives. The food is served to guests from platters and, in some instances, some of the food is prepared at the table. This type of service requires more space between tables and some level of skill on the part of the servers.

Usually, the decision on the food service types is based on the buyer's preference, but the other factors listed above may limit choices. The sales manager or services manager should explain the advantages and disadvantages of each service type to the prospective buyers.

Food and Beverage Pricing

The prices for food and beverage service are normally included on a series of menus that are placed in the sales packets distributed by most hospitality firms. In some cases, hospitality organizations do not deviate from the listed prices, while in other cases, sales managers are given some latitude for negotiating prices. The following is a list of questions that need to be addressed when determining actual payment.

What records will be used to determine the payment for meals? A method must be chosen to determine the volume, or the amount of usage. Some of the more common methods are:

◆ *Distributing tickets that are collected by the servers.* The final count can be determined when things are not as busy, and the group is only charged for what is actually consumed.

◆ *Counting heads during the function.* This can be done while the guests are seated. However, the count is performed amidst the confusion of serving the guests and can be open to error.

◆ *The kitchen counts the number of plates that are prepared and distributed.* Once again, the group is only charged for what is actually consumed, but there may be some confusion trying to count while there is a lot of commotion in the kitchen.

◆ *Charge the group for the actual quantities that are consumed.* The payment is based on what is used from the inventory and can be tied closely to cost; is easy to calculate the profitability of the function.

How many servers will be provided? This decision is often left to the hospitality firm, but it may depend on union regulations. The number of servers is based on the size of the function, the room setup, and the type of food service. There are rules of thumb that can be followed (for example, one bartender for every 100 guests). The banquet captain and services manager are experienced in determining the right number, but it also depends on the availability of part-time employees. Therefore, the actual ratio of servers to guests might vary by event, regardless of size, service type, and room setup.

How should the group be charged for beverages? The prices for beverages are determined ahead of time, but a method must be agreed upon for calculating the actual usage. Following is a list of common approaches

- *Charge a fixed fee, or package rate, per person.* This amount is based on the average number of drinks consumed by the average person in a given time period.
- *Charge by the drink.* This method is fair for both the hotel and the group, but it requires the bartenders to keep track while they are busy serving. This approach is easier to use when point-of-sale systems are available at the site of the function.
- *Charge by the can or the bottle.* This method can be used for refreshment breaks or meals when everything is served in cans or bottles, however, it can't be used when drinks are being poured (e.g., mixed drinks or iced tea). When used, this method allows the count to be performed after the event, based on the beginning inventory.

How should hors d'oeuvres be charged? There are three basic approaches for charging groups for hors d'oeuvres.

- **Charge per person per hour.** This is based on the average amount of food the average person will consume per hour. It is an easy method as long as an accurate head count can be determined.
- **Charge by the table or tray.** If guests are seated, then you can serve the same amount of hors d'oeuvres per table. Otherwise, it may be easier to charge for the number of trays served at the agreed upon price per tray (there may be more than one variety or price level of hors d'oeuvres).
- **Charge by the piece.** This may be the most accurate method, but it is also the most time consuming.

What other costs should be considered? There may be some additional costs that, if overlooked, could cost the hospitality firm money.

- *Taxes.* The hospitality company must pay tax on its revenues and must make sure to include tax in the pricing scheme. Some hospitality orgnizations' menu prices include the tax while others do not. It is important to make it clear to the meeting planners to avoid confusion or dissatisfaction.
- *Gratuities.* Tips or gratuities are normally charged in addition to the food and beverage prices. In some cases, they are at the discretion of the buyer, but hospitality firms that are unionized

must require a certain amount (such as 17 to 20 percent) regardless of the level of service. This should be made clear.

- ◆ *Surcharges.* Prospective buyers should be made aware of any other charges that are not included in the price. There are instances where hospitality firms incur additional charges that need to be passed on to the consumer.

- ◆ *Corkage fees.* Some hospitality firms allow groups to supply their own beverages, but local and state laws may require a corkage fee, which is a fee charged to open the bottle on site.

Audiovisual Equipment

A service that is often required during meetings is the use of audiovisual (A-V) equipment. Hotels generally have a price list included in the buyer's guide that describes the equipment that is available for rental. The sales manager will normally have more flexibility in pricing A-V equipment when it is owned by the hospitality organization and not leased.

These advantages are similar to the typical "rent" or "own" comparisons made for many products. In general, there is a trade-off between risk and return. As your potential return increases, it is accompanied by an increase in the risk of loss or failure. The hospitality firm's A-V equipment needs will affect the decision whether to own or use for lease equipment.

Most corporate buyers or meeting planners use the basic types of A-V equipment on a regular basis, but the need may arise to request equipment that is not as common. For instance, more groups are now using teleconferencing and satellite hookups. However, most hospitality firms cannot justify owning the equipment, given the low number of requests they receive for this type of equipment. Therefore, another alternative is to own or lease or rent the other types of equipment on an as-needed basis. The most commonly used types of A-V equipment are slide projectors, overhead projectors, video projectors, and flip charts/chalkboards.

Slide projectors are popular among many presenters because they provide good color reproduction, are capable of projecting a large image, and offer the advantage of remote operation. The speaker can face the audience and walk around the room during the presentation. A data projector is another form of slide projector that allows speakers to use computers in their presentations. Data projectors make it possible to use motion in the presentation, whereas slide projectors are limited in this respect. However, both types of equipment can be noisy because of the fans.

Overhead projectors are still standard at conferences and meetings. Overhead presentations are easy to prepare and the machines are simple to operate. The speaker can face the crowd and make additions by marking or highlighting the overhead transparency. The other advantage that overhead projectors have over slide projectors and data projectors is that the room does not have to be completely dark to see the presentation. However, the color reproduction is not as clear as that of the other projectors and they also have the fan noise.

Video projectors can be used to make full-motion and color presentations. They also have some computer capability and are relatively easy to operate. Another advantage is that you can easily "playback" part of the presentation if necessary. However, depending on the size of the television, or projection screen, the size of the audience may be limited. Also, there is still no one standard format for tapes.

Flip charts and chalkboards represent one of the earliest, most basic forms of A-V equipment. They are inexpensive, the presentation can be spontaneous, and there usually is not a seating problem. However, the size of the audience is limited and it can be messy to erase or cross out unwanted materials.

Regardless of the type of A-V equipment being used, it is important to ensure that the best sight lines are available for session participants. The best position for placing screens or flip charts is in the corner of the room, preferably away from the door. The presenter can stand on one side of the screen or flip chart without blocking the audience's view. Unfortunately, some hospitality firms have fixed equipment that cannot be moved and it tends to be in the center of the wall.

Exhibit Space

Some conventions and conferences require exhibit space so that members or attendees can view displays of various products or services. Large conventions often include trade shows where suppliers display their newest products and features. When corporate meetings reserve exhibit space, it is billed directly to the company. When association meetings reserve exhibit space, the association is charged. However, the association often resells the space to potential exhibitors in an effort to make some profit. The following steps show the normal procedure used by associations in securing exhibit space.

1. The association contracts with the hospitality firm for exhibit space.

2. The association solicits exhibitors and contracts with them for booth space.

3. The association contracts with a decorator to coordinate the overall exhibit and follow hotel guidelines.

4. The decorators send information to the individual exhibitors and work with them on their booths.

5. The booth locations are assigned and the floor plan is submitted to the local fire department for its final approval.

The amount the group is charged depends on a variety of factors. Initial prices can be adjusted after considering the group's guest room and meeting room commitments, the expected food and beverage revenues, the group's potential for repeat business, the other demands for the space, and the total square footage required. In addition, the hospitality firm should consider any special problems that could be related to the group's use of the exhibit space. For example, some trade exhibits require 24-hour security because of the value, or sensitive nature, of the materials. The hospitality facility may choose to supply the additional security for a certain fee, or may require the group to find its own security. The firm's policy on security and its liability should be made clear in the contract.

Key Concepts

Chapter 12 focuses on servicing the meeting after the sale is made. There are a number of issues to consider, starting with the decision of when to make the transition from the hotel sales department to the conference services department. There are three points at which a transition can be made:

- during the site inspection
- immediately after signing the contract
- one year before the meeting

There are four possible methods for making room reservations depending upon the type of meeting and who is responsible for making the payment:

- postal reply cards
- rooming lists
- toll-free numbers
- city housing bureaus

Function room assignments are based on the type of setup and the type of food service. The three most popular meeting room setups are:

- auditorium or theater style
- schoolroom style
- boardroom or conference style

The most popular types of food service are:

- plate service
- pre-set service
- buffet style
- platter service
- European service

The following questions are used to determine the actual payment for food and beverage functions:

- What records will be used to determine the payment for meals?
- How many servers will be provided?
- How should the group be charged for beverages?
- How should hors d'oeuvres be charged?
- What other costs should be considered?

Finally, the conference services personnel must take care of audiovisual requirements and work with the group on exhibit space if there is going to be a display area or trade show.

PERSONAL SELLING TOOLS

here are a number of tools that can be developed and used by salespeople to improve their performance. These tools increase the efficiency and effectiveness of sales presentations. This chapter discusses two such tools: time management and negotiating skills. In addition, salespeople should conduct business in an ethical manner. The last section in this chapter discusses ethical issues faced by salespeople in an attempt to form some basic guidelines.

Time Management

Time is a critical resource for salespeople because it is limited and must be managed properly to ensure efficient and effective performance. Figure 13-1 displays a general breakdown of the normal activities in a salesperson's day and the time spent on each activity.

As you can see, only a small percentage of time is actually spent selling. Therefore, in an attempt to maximize the time when one is engaged in selling, it is important to understand the concept of time management.

Time management can be thought of as a process, or a cycle, as shown in Figure 13-2. First, salespeople set their goals in accordance with the expectations of the firm. Second, once the goals are set, salespeople must develop sales strategies and allocate resources. The third stage involves the actual implementation of the strategies. Finally, it is necessary to evaluate or measure performance based on the goals that are initially set.

Setting Sales Goals

The first step in the time-management process is to set sales goals. A salesperson's goals will be a direct extension of his or her overall lifestyle and career goals. Therefore, it is important to understand

Activity	Percentage of Time
Travel	25-30%
Waiting	20-25%
Paperwork	20-25%
Casual conversation	5-10%
Selling	20-25%

Figure 13-1 A Salesperson's Day

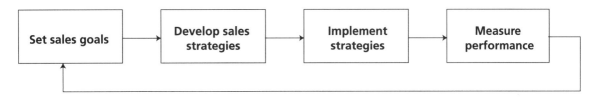

Figure 13-2 Time Management Cycle

the personal side of the individual, as well as his or her career plans. For example, an individual who has a family may not want to travel overnight as often as someone who is single, or the individual might be willing to forego additional income in return for more time to spend with his or her family.

Basically, sales goals can be placed into three categories: conversion, sales achievement, and sales activities. Conversion goals deal with the salesperson's ability to obtain commitment in the process of making sales calls to new prospects and existing accounts. Sales achievement or performance goals are based on actual volume or revenue that the salesperson acquires. Finally, sales activities goals are concerned with the number and mix of sales calls, and the ability to schedule actual sales presentations. These goals should be clear and concise, quantifiable, and specify a time frame. This will make it much easier to evaluate and measure performance.

Developing Sales Strategies

There is a rule that has been applied in marketing for some time, called the 80/20 rule. This proposition holds that 80 percent of profitable business will be generated by 20 percent of the customers. This rule was found to hold true for many tangible products, but it would seem to apply to services as well. In particular, hospitality firms segment customers based on their frequency of use with the firm's frequent flier, frequent guest, and frequent diner programs. Those who purchase more, receive more benefits and attention. There is no difference when it comes to group business sales.

Not all prospects, guests, or meeting planners should be treated equally. Rather, special attention should be given to those who produce the largest share of the revenue and profits or who have the potential to do so. The groups that make up this 20 percent are termed **key accounts**. They deserve special attention and extra-personalized selling efforts.

Sales and marketing departments should keep a close watch on the level of business provided by each account. Trends should be studied to determine which accounts are growing and which are declining. An analysis of each account should be conducted periodically to determine the total revenue and contribution margin for each account. Based on this analysis, accounts can be classified as shown in Figure 13-3.

Those accounts with the highest profit margins and best potential for increased business must be given extra attention, while those that are marginal should not consume too much of sales managers' time and effort. Keep in mind that resources are limited and that they should be directed toward the accounts with the most profit potential.

	High Profit Margin	Low Profit Margin
High Potential for Increased Business	desirable accounts	undeveloped accounts
Low Potential for Increased Business	developed accounts	undesirable accounts

Figure 13-3 Account Classification Grid

Desirable Accounts. These are the accounts with high profit margins and good potential for increased business. Desirable accounts should receive a high level of attention in the form of sales calls and account maintenance because they are the organization's most attractive accounts. These accounts represent a large portion of the hospitality firm's source of funds. Therefore, it is important that the firm allocate an adequate level of resources to continue developing these accounts.

Developed Accounts. These are the accounts with high profit margins, but not high potential for increased business. Developed accounts provide a steady stream of cash flow, but there is not much potential for increasing the level of cash flow. Currently, the firm's strategy should be to allocate the resources necessary to maintain these accounts in order to ensure future business. However, it is important that salespeople are careful not to spend an excessive amount of their time on these accounts.

Undeveloped Accounts. These are the accounts with low profit margins and good potential for increased business. The firm currently has a weak position with these accounts, but there is an opportunity to improve this position. The strategy should be to allocate a fairly large amount of resources to develop these accounts, even though they don't provide much cash flow at present.

Undesirable Accounts. These are the accounts with low profit margins and little potential for increased business. Currently, the firm has a weak position and the accounts offer little opportunity for future cash flow. Therefore, the strategy should be to allocate a minimal amount of resources and to give consideration to eliminating the business all together. Another alternative is to shift the attention from high effort in the form of personal sales calls toward lower effort in the form of telephone calls and direct mail.

The grid helps salespeople classify their existing accounts based on the hospitality firm's competitive position with an account and the account's future sales potential. All firms have some limitations in terms of resources, including the amount of time salespeople have to call on existing accounts and develop new business. It is important that salespeople manage their time so that they can maintain existing accounts, while at the same time, continually develop new business to increase the sales base and compensate for accounts that are lost or decreasing in revenue.

Implementing Sales Strategies

Once the sales strategies have been developed, the next step is to implement them. At this stage, it is important to plan the activities that will be pursued. First, the salesperson should make a list of the activities to be performed. Second, the salesperson should prioritize the activities based on their importance in achieving the sales goals. Third, the salesperson should estimate the amount of time each activity will consume. Fourth, the salesperson should develop a time schedule that can be followed in performing the activities. Finally, the salesperson should monitor any variances in the budgeted time and the actual time that it takes to perform the activities. This will allow the salesperson to make adjustments along the way.

Following is a list of potential "time traps" that result in wasting a salesperson's time, which in turn leads to inefficiency and ineffectiveness.

- *Calling on unqualified or unprofitable prospects.* It is important for salespeople to determine the ability and willingness of prospects to buy their products and services. Also, the accounts must be profitable enough to justify the use of firm resources. It is possible that accounts can be profitable without meeting minimum levels for firm performance. These problems can be avoided by properly qualifying prospects before allocating any significant time or resources to making sales calls.

- *Performing tasks that could be delegated.* Many firms benefit from specialization of labor, and salespeople are best utilized for selling. Other duties can be delegated to other members in the sales department. Most hotel sales departments have sales assistants and other support personnel.

- *Insufficiently planning each day's activities.* Each afternoon, salespeople should make a schedule for the next day. Travel plans should be arranged in an attempt to minimize the time between sales calls. Also, tasks should be prioritized and planned around necessary time constraints.

- *Making poor use of time between sales calls.* Modern technology has provided mobile equipment, such as telephones and laptops that allows salespeople to perform traditional office tasks while away from the office.

- *Making too many cold calls.* Once again, it is important for salespeople to balance their time between existing accounts and new business. Although some degree of cold calling is required, when attempting to develop new business, the potential for success is improved when salespeople take the time to qualify accounts and set up appointments rather than relying primarily on cold calls.

- *Being disorganized.* Salespeople should keep organized records and use an efficient filing system because of a great deal of time can be wasted trying to find documents. Electronic organizers and computers are helpful, but there is still a need for actual paper copies of contracts and memos.

◆ *Taking long lunches and too many coffee breaks.* It is easy to get sidetracked when socializing with fellow workers and friends. Leaving the office or walking away from one's desk can result in significant periods of down time. A certain level of break time is beneficial; however, at some point it becomes counterproductive.

◆ *Spending too much time entertaining prospects and customers.* It is important to build relationships and give customers personal attention. However, it is easy to get carried away and to be excessive, especially when it comes to entertaining. This does not refer just to the recreational act of entertaining, it also refers to giving property tours and speaking on the telephone. Salespeople have a finite number of working hours and they need to manage those hours properly. The more time spent with any one customer or prospect, the less time left for others.

◆ *Procrastinating on major projects or difficult tasks.* Salespeople can reduce large undertakings into smaller, manageable tasks that can be readily accomplished. It is easy to "spin your wheels" when you agonize over a complicated task involving a large time commitment.

◆ *Conducting unnecessary meetings, visits, and telephone calls.* Once again, there is only so much time in the day and it must be used effectively. Meetings should not be scheduled until everyone is fully prepared, and visits and telephone calls should have a specific purpose with a desired outcome.

◆ *Trying to do too many things at one time.* It is often better to concentrate on one task until it is finished. Taking calls during a meeting or while preparing a contract can lead to delays and other problems. Under some circumstances, it may be necessary to eliminate possible interruptions.

Measuring Performance

After sales goals are set, strategies are developed, and resources are allocated, it is necessary to measure performance to determine if the time-management process is effective. It is important to look at various measures of performance to correctly assess the effectiveness of the process. The performance measures should be consistent with the sales goals.

Conversion Rate. One type of performance measure is to look at the number of accounts that are sold in relation to the number of sales calls that are made. This measure can be dissected further by customer type (corporate, association), size of account (number of room nights, total revenue), and/or level of services (guest rooms, meeting rooms, and food and beverage).

Sales Achievement. One way to measure the salesperson's performance is in relation to his or her goals. In other words, what are the actual sales, in volume or dollar value, in relation to the goals or quotas set for that salesperson? Is the salesperson meeting his or her goals, exceeding them or falling short of them? Normally, when a salesperson meets his or her quota, it is raised for the next year. If the quota is not met, it is necessary to examine the situation and determine why. Another variation of this measure would be to look at the level of commissions the salesperson has received. Once again, these measures can be segmented by customer type, size of the account, or the level of services.

Sales Activities. The final category for measuring performance would be to analyze the actual sales calls. Sales goals may focus on the number, or percentage, of new account calls. The salesperson's time must be allocated between existing accounts and developing new business. For example, how many cold calls are made per week or per month? How many sales presentations are actually performed?

Negotiating Skills

In today's environment, salespeople should be ready to negotiate with buyers from both consumer and industrial markets. There is a proliferation of information available to consumers, including tips and suggestions for getting the "best deals" from manufacturers and retailers. Advances in technology make this information easy to access, thereby allowing consumers to compare alternatives with minimal information research. The negotiation process is particularly critical in industrial markets because of the high volume. For example, if a hotel sales manager is negotiating the room rate for 500 rooms over four nights (2,000 room nights), a reduction of $5 in price results in a decrease in revenue of $10,000. This transaction could take place over a matter of seconds.

The goal of any negotiation is to achieve a win-win situation. It is important not to take the negotiation process as a competition because someone will end up losing. Dissatisfied customers do not return, and they provide negative word of mouth to their colleagues. Rather, it is important to create an exchange that results in the involved parties' mutual satisfaction. A good sales manager will plan for the sales presentation and the inevitable negotiation process. A complete knowledge of the competitive environment will provide useful parameters for steering the negotiations. In addition, the sales manager should develop acceptable ranges and options for negotiating to ensure profitability. The following tips will improve the sales manager's potential for success in negotiating.[1]

- *When you give something up, try to gain something in return*. Once you show a tendency to negotiate, prospects will try to negotiate on every item. Therefore, make it clear that you expect something in return for making concessions. For example, a hotel sales manager could say "I'll lower the room rate by $5 per night if you guarantee 100 rooms for 4 nights."
- *Do not make too many concessions at an early stage*. Once a salesperson starts to make concessions it becomes contagious. The buyer will realize that concessions can be made and will try to negotiate every little component of the service. Therefore, it is advisable to postpone some issues until later in the negotiations, after most of the decisions are made.
- *Look for items other than price to negotiate*. As mentioned earlier, a small reduction in price could result in a large decrease in revenue when dealing with volume business. Sales managers can focus on items other than room rates. For example, planners could be given free meeting space, room upgrades, reduced meal prices, or free audiovisual equipment. All of these items would

have a much smaller impact on the hotel's bottom line and they provide buyers with a sense of accomplishment.

◆ *Do not attack your prospect's demand; look for the motive behind it.* Try not to tell a prospect that his or her demand is ridiculous or unreasonable. This will only anger the prospect and have a negative impact on the negotiations. Instead, remain calm and ask the prospect to explain the reason for making such a demand. For example, if a meeting planner asks for a very low room rate it may be because of a small, or restricted, budget.

◆ *Do not defend your position; ask for feedback and advice from the prospect.* If you meet resistance to your offer, don't become defensive. Simply ask the prospect why he or she thinks that it is unreasonable. Asking, "What would you do if you were in my position?" is often beneficial in this situation.

The more sales calls you make, the more knowledgeable you become regarding the "do's" and "don'ts" of negotiation. Hopefully, this learning process will not cost your firm too much along the way.

It is also important to recognize any unhelpful behaviors being exhibited by the buyers. Common problems you could encounter are buyers' becoming confused or indecisive. In addition, buyers may become emotional or aggressive in their behavior. The table in Figure 13-4 lists these problem areas and provides possible solutions for each area.

Problems	Possible Solutions
Confused buyer	◆ Use visual aids to clarify complex issues. ◆ Put proposals in writing using clear and concise language. ◆ Use a step-by-step agenda to avoid confusion.
Indecisive buyer	◆ Proceed slowly and methodically; repeat important points. ◆ Promise to review the issues at a later time. ◆ Try to present the issues in an original manner.
Aggressive buyer	◆ Repeat the facts, keeping calm and avoid emotional language. ◆ Refuse to be drawn into an argument, or battle. ◆ Suggest a recess if things get too emotional and heated.
Emotional buyer	◆ Don't challenge the motives or integrity of the buyer. ◆ Don't interrupt outbursts, be patient and wait to respond. ◆ Try to be rational and use logic; recess, if necessary.

Figure 13-4 Common Problems

Ethical Issues in Personal Selling

As with most other areas of business, there is also the potential for unethical behavior by salespeople. Firms' policies and practices should provide salespeople with a good understanding of allowable behavior or conduct. When these policies are written and used in training, salespeople are more likely to adhere to the firm's ethical standards. The following is a brief description of the most common types of *unethical* behavior among salespeople.

- *Sharing confidential information.* Salespeople and customers build close relationships over time that lead to the disclosure of confidential information based on trust. There is a potential for salespeople to share this information with customers' competitors, either voluntarily or involuntarily. Salespeople need to be cognizant of this possible breach and realize that it may backfire. This behavior speaks to the character of the salespeople.

- *Reciprocity.* This refers to the mutual exchange of benefits between buyers and sellers. If a firm has a policy of reciprocity, this can be viewed as an exclusive tying arrangement, which is illegal. For example, the case where a hotel may only purchase supplies from firms that agree to use its services for corporate travel.

- *Bribery.* Bribes in the form of monetary payoffs or kickbacks are unethical, if not illegal. Many U.S. firms find themselves at a disadvantage in international markets when their corporate policies, and U.S. laws, forbid them from engaging in the practice of offering bribes in countries where it is accepted as a normal business practice. Some meeting planners have coerced hotels into giving them kickbacks from the room revenues for their meetings.

- *Gift giving and entertainment.* There is a fine line between gift giving, entertainment, and bribery. If the gift is being used to obtain the customer's business, then it amounts to a bribe. Gifts should only be given after contracts are signed as a symbol of the firm's gratitude. Meeting planners are inundated with gifts in the form of hotel coupons and frequent guest points, or even frequent flier miles. Also, "wining and dining" clients is a popular sales technique. "Fam," or familiarization, trips provide meeting planners and travel agents with free hotel rooms, airline travel, and entrance to tourist attractions or special events. In response, some firms have policies regarding the acceptance of gifts and entertainment by meeting planners and travel agents.

- *Making misleading sales claims.* In their pursuit of sales and quotas, salespeople may decide to provide customers or prospects with misleading information. It is not uncommon in hotel sales for sales managers to promise meeting planners' items that the food and beverage department cannot deliver. This results in some difficult negotiations at the time of the meeting. Another misleading practice is *blind cutting*, which was discussed in Chapter 11.

◈ *Business defamation.* Salespeople sometimes make disparaging comments about their competitors when dealing with customers. Not only does this reflect poorly on the salespeople and their firms, but, in some instances, it is actually illegal (slander or libel). It is very tempting to take a "cheap shot" at a competitor when making comparisons between properties or firms. However, salespeople should constrain themselves to answering specific questions with factual information.

The extent to which a firm is successful in deterring unethical behavior on the part of its employees will depend on the firm's treatment of employees who violate its policies and the level of support for the policies throughout the organization.

Key Concepts

Chapter 13 presents some personal selling tools that could be used by salespeople to improve their performance. There is also a discussion of ethics in personal selling.

Time management
◈ setting sales goals
◈ developing sales strategies
◈ implementing sales strategies
◈ measuring performance

Negotiating skills
◈ When you give something up, try to gain something in return.
◈ Do not make too many concessions at an early stage.
◈ Look for items other than price to negotiate.
◈ Do not attack your prospect's demand—look for the motive behind it.
◈ Do not defend your position—ask for feedback and advice from the prospect.

Ethical issues
◈ sharing confidential information
◈ reciprocity, mutual exchange of benefits
◈ bribery
◈ gift giving and entertainment
◈ making misleading sales claims
◈ business defamation

Endnotes

[1] Futrell, Charles M., (1996) *Fundamentals of Selling: Customers for Life*, Chicago, IL: The McGraw-Hill Companies, Inc., 243.

14

REVENUE MANAGEMENT AND PRICE NEGOTIATION

R evenue management is a concept concerned with selling the right product to the right customer for the right price at the right time, thereby maximizing the firm's revenue.[1] In other words, revenue management refers to a technique used to maximize the revenue, or yield, obtained from a services operation, given limited capacity and uneven demand. In fact, **yield management** is the term often used by airlines and hotels to describe the revenue management process. Within the hospitality and tourism industry, yield management has come into more widespread use with the expansion of computerized property management systems. In its most basic form, yield management utilizes a firm's historical data to predict the demand for future sales, with the goal of setting prices that will maximize the firm's revenue and profit.

Revenue Management

Revenue management is a valuable tool within the hospitality and travel industry for several reasons:[2]

- *Perishable inventory.* Most hospitality and travel services are perishable. If a hotel room is not occupied one evening, or an airline flies with empty seats, the potential revenue for those services cannot be captured at a later date. Similarly, catering facilities and meeting space represent perishable inventory for a lodging, meeting, or food service facility.
- *Fluctuating demand.* Most hospitality and travel firms experience demand that rises and falls within a day, week, month, or year. During high demand periods, services are sold at or near full price. During the low demand, or non-peak periods, capacity is left unused.
- *Ability to segment customers.* Firms must be able to segment customers based on price and offer a discounted price to a selective group of customers. In other words, the various customer segments must have different price sensitivities and economic values for the same type of product or service.
- *Low variable costs.* Hospitality and travel firms often have a large ratio of fixed to variable costs, which would favor a high volume strategy. The marginal cost of serving an additional customer is minimal as long as there is excess capacity.

If consumers could not be segmented based on price and economic value, then firms could employ a mass marketing strategy with one basic marketing program for all consumers.

Selective Discounting

One of the cornerstones of yield management is the ability to offer discounts to only a select group of customers. Rather than offer one price for a given time period, either peak or non-peak, firms are able to discriminate between consumers. This minimizes the effect of lost revenue resulting from consumers paying a discounted price when they would have willingly paid full price. In order to accomplish this, service firms normally place restrictions on the discounted price so that consumers must sacrifice something in return for the discount. For example, catering facilities and hotels can require a minimum amount of revenue or volume, or require guests to book during off-peak times.

Historical Analysis

One of the major problems facing service firms using revenue management systems is the determination of the amount of capacity to make available at the discounted rate. As mentioned earlier, yield management makes use of historical data in predicting future trends. The historical booking curve can be constructed using data from the same period in the previous year, and adjusting for recent trends seen in the most recent periods. The curve can be used to compare current reservations with historical patterns in an effort to monitor room rates and pricing strategies. The curve in Figure 14-1 illustrates a typical pattern for a large conference hotel.

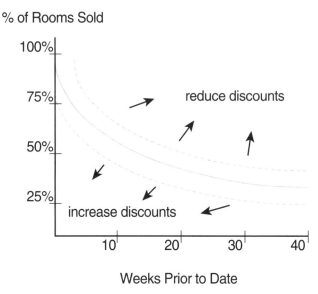

Figure 14-1 Historical Booking Curve

The solid line in the graph represents the historical pattern for room sales prior to the date in question. In general, the hotel would determine a comfort zone and construct a confidence interval around the actual occupancy rate. If prior sales are within this interval, then the hotel continues using its current discounting policy. If the occupancy rate exceeds the upper level, then the hotel will temporarily reduce the number of discounted rooms and rates. If the occupancy rate falls below the lower level, then the hotel will offer more discounted rooms and rates until the occupancy rate is brought back within the predicted interval.

Hotel sales departments are given room allotments based on past history. Within these allotments, the sales staff must determine the allowable price range for each group based on the total potential revenue from all sources such as guest rooms, meeting room rental, and food and beverage. Rental car companies and airlines perform a similar analysis and set rates based on the relationship between current demand and historical demand. Finally, catering facilities must also manage the ratio of actual revenue to potential revenue when they sell their services in advance. It may be prudent to turn down a piece of business if history would suggest that you might have other opportunities at a higher rate or overall potential revenue.

Revenue Management Equation

As stated earlier, the goal of revenue management is to maximize the revenue, or yield, from a service operation. The following equation is a simplified version of the calculation used in actual programs.

$$\text{Maximize}\left(\frac{\text{Actual Revenue}}{\text{Potential Revenue}}\right)$$

The potential revenue for a hotel would be the number of total rooms available for sale multiplied by the rack rate for those rooms. For instance, if a hotel had 200 rooms that all had a rack rate of $100, the potential room revenue for that hotel would be $20,000 per night. However, if the hotel had an occupancy rate of 70 percent and an average room rate of $80, then the actual revenue would be $11,200 [(0.7 × 200) × $80]. The yield in this case would be 0.56 ($11,200/$20,000). The goal is to maximize this figure, or get as close to 1.0 as possible. What if this hotel would have offered more discounts and had an occupancy rate of 80 percent and an average room rate of $75? The actual revenue would have been $12,000 [(0.8 × 200) × $75], or a yield of .60 ($12,000/$20,000). As you can see, the potential revenue remains the same, but the actual revenue will change depending on the level of discounts and the price sensitivity of consumers.

This example is overly simplified in order to demonstrate the basic use of yield management. In reality, hotels have different rooms with different rack rates, and many different market segments, including business and pleasure transients, and various group markets. Each of these major segments can be divided into smaller subsets. For instance, the group market can be segmented into association, corporate, and incentive travel. Hotels have created positions and, in some cases, departments that are responsible for revenue management. These individuals perform historical booking analysis and confer with the hotel's executive committee to determine discounting policies.

Another area that needs to be considered in determining a hotel's discounting policy is the additional revenue that is generated from guests other than the room revenue. For example, hotels can earn additional revenue from guests in the restaurant, the bar, fitness centers, parking, laundry services, room service, corporate services such as faxing and shipping, and by catering for groups. Rather than analyze each individual guest, hotels look at the major market segments and calculate a "multiplier" that can be used to adjust room revenue for additional revenue potential. This is important because hotels must maximize the revenue they receive from all sources. For instance, it would be a mistake to take a transient guest who paid $10 more a night than a business traveler, if the business traveler is likely to spend more than $10 a day for additional services. Similarly, turning down a group because of high demand among transient customers may result in a loss of revenue from catering services that would have been purchased by the group. However, in high peak demand seasons, such as fall in New England, hotels can charge considerably more to transient customers than groups and it would be a mistake to book a group well in advance and forego this additional revenue.

Revenue management has had a major impact on the hospitality and travel industry. The advances in computer technology have improved the ability to estimate demand and revenue. In addition, it has become easier to segment markets and employ selective discounting through vehicles such as the Internet. In the future, revenue management programs will become more affordable to smaller operations. In fact, simple yield management models can be developed using a common spreadsheet program.

Revenue Management and Group Displacement

Probably the most difficult decision that a hotel needs to make is when to turn away business. With a limited amount of capacity, salespeople may need to choose between two different accounts, or turn down an account because there is a good probability that the hotel will be able to obtain a more profitable account for the same time period. This is the major challenge of revenue management— **group displacement**. Who do you accept and at what rate? It is easy to take the safe approach and book the first group that meets your minimum standards ("a bird in the hand is worth two in the bush"). However, the hotel may have been able to make more money had it waited.

As an illustration of this point, one of the authors waited until the last minute to make plans for the New York Hotel Show during a year in which the New York Marathon was being held at the same time. Needless to say, many of the city's hotels were "sold out" of rooms. After calling around, it was interesting that most of the area properties of the Marriott chain still had rooms available. At first glance, one might assume that the chain had obtained its fair share. However, upon further examination, it is clear that the Marriott utilizes an effective revenue management program. The other hotels booked their rooms as early as possible at a target rate. In contrast, Marriott based its decision on demand and was able to sell its remaining rooms at the highest rate possible, thereby increasing its revenue per available room (REVPAR) and average daily rate.

Assume for example that you have a 500-room hotel with a corporate rate of $150 and a potential group willing to pay $100. Given the following occupancy and group pattern, calculate the revenue gain (loss) per day and the overall effect of displacement (note: displacement = revenue gained revenue lost).

	Monday	Tuesday	Wednesday	Thursday
Occupancy rate	80%	100%	95%	85%
Group pattern (rooms)	50	100	100	100
Revenue gain (loss)	$_____	_____	_____	_____
Displacement	$_____	_____	_____	_____

What is your decision? Do you turn down the group or displace the corporate travelers?

_____

What other factors should be considered when making this kind of decision?

_____

Setting Prices

Once a firm's pricing objectives are set, it is necessary to identify the role that price will serve in the product's overall marketing strategy. Price can be set high to restrict the firm's market to a limited segment of buyers (such as luxury hotels and their upscale catering departments), set low to attract buyers (such as economy hotels), or kept neutral to emphasize other aspects of marketing (e.g., midscale hotels and large contract food service firms). *Economic value* can be defined as the sum of a product's *reference value*, or the cost of the competing product that the consumer perceives as the closest substitute, and a product's *differentiation value*, or the value to the consumer (both positive and negative) of any differences between a firm's offering and the reference product.

When management establishes prices, three approaches can be used either individually or in combination with one another. The three approaches are: (1) cost-oriented pricing, (2) demand-oriented pricing, and (3) competitive pricing.

Cost-Oriented Pricing

As the name implies, cost-oriented pricing uses a firm's cost to provide a product or service as a basis for pricing. In general, firms want to set a price high enough to cover costs and make a profit. There are two types of costs that can be considered: (1) fixed costs and (2) variable costs. Fixed costs are incurred by a company when it goes into business and they do not vary with changes in sales volume. For example, food service providers must invest in a building, kitchen equipment, and tables before they even begin to serve customers. Variable costs are associated with doing business, and they vary with changes in sales volume. For example, food service operations incur costs for food, labor, and cleaning that are directly related to the level of sales.

Breakeven analysis can be used to examine the relationships between costs, sales, and profits. The breakeven point (BEP) is the point where total revenue and total cost are equal. In other words, the BEP in units would be the number of units that must be sold at a given contribution margin (price–variable cost) to cover the firm's total fixed costs:

$$BEP_{units} = \frac{\text{Total fixed costs}}{(\text{Selling price} - \text{Variable cost})}$$

The BEP in dollars can be calculated by multiplying the BEP in units by the selling price per unit. Breakeven analysis is a seemingly easy method for analyzing potential pricing strategies, however, one must be careful to use only costs that are relevant to the decision so that the results are accurate.

Figure 14-2 illustrates the relationships between costs, sales, and profits. As mentioned above, fixed costs are those costs that are incurred regardless of sales. Therefore, they remain constant with changes in sales volume and are represented by a horizontal line. The total cost line intersects the fixed cost line where it begins on the vertical axis and increases with volume to account for variable costs. The total revenue line begins at the origin and increases with volume. The BEP in units is the point where the total revenue line intersects with the total cost line. When firms operate at volumes less than the BEP, losses are incurred because total revenue is not enough to cover the total cost of producing and marketing the product. When volume exceeds the BEP, firms will make a profit because total revenue exceeds total cost.

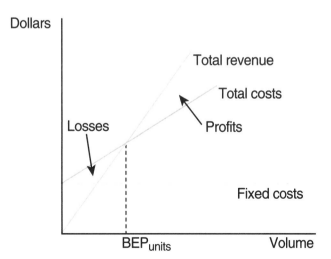

Figure 14-2 Breakeven Analysis

However, breakeven analysis does not account for the price sensitivity of consumers or the competition. In addition, it is very important that the costs used in the analysis are accurate. Any changes in the contribution margin or fixed costs can have a significant impact on the BEP. Finally, the breakeven formula can be easily adjusted to account for a desired amount of profit. The desired amount of profit would be added to the numerator (total fixed costs) and would represent the additional number of units that would need to be sold at the current contribution margin to cover the desired amount.

Cost-plus pricing is the most basic approach to pricing in the industry. The price for a product or service is determined by adding a desired mark-up to the cost of producing and marketing the item. The mark-up is in the form of a percentage and price is set using the following equation:

$$Price = ATC + m(ATC)$$

where: ATC = the average total cost per unit
           m = the mark-up percentage/100%

The average total cost per unit is calculated by adding the variable cost per unit to the fixed cost per unit. The fixed cost per unit is simply the total fixed costs divided by the number of units sold.

The cost-plus pricing approach is popular because it is simple to use and it focuses on covering costs and making a profit. However, management must have a good understanding of the firm's costs in order to price effectively. Some costs are truly fixed, while other costs may be semi-fixed. Semi-fixed costs are fixed over a certain range of sales, but vary when sales go outside that range. In addition to the problem of determining the relevant costs, the cost-plus approach ignores consumer demand and the competition. This may cause a firm to charge too high, or too low, of a price.

Target-return pricing is another form of cost-oriented pricing that sets price to yield a target rate of return on a firm's investment. This approach is more sophisticated than the cost-plus approach because it focuses on an overall rate of return for the business rather than a desired profit per unit. The target-return price can be calculated using the following equation:

$$Price = ATC + (desired\ dollar\ return/unit\ sales)$$

The average total cost per unit is determined the same way as in the cost-plus approach, and it is increased by the dollar return per unit necessary to provide the target rate of return. Hotels can use target return pricing to determine a target revenue per available room (REVPAR) for guest rooms. It is also common to want to generate a certain return per square foot of meeting space. This approach is also relatively simple, but it still ignores competitors' prices and consumer demand.

Demand-Oriented Pricing

Demand-oriented pricing makes use of consumer perceptions of value as a basis for setting prices. The goal of this pricing approach is to set prices to capture more value, not to maximize volume. A price is charged that will allow the firm to extract the most consumer surplus from the market based on the *reservation price*, which is the maximum price that a consumer is willing to pay for a product or service. This price can be difficult to determine unless management has a firm grasp of the price sensitivity of consumers. Economists measure price sensitivity using the **price elasticity of demand**, which is the percentage change in quantity demanded divided by the percentage change in price. Assuming an initial price of P_1 and an initial quantity of Q_1, the price elasticity of demand (ε_p) for a change in price from P_1 to P_2 can be calculated by:

$$\varepsilon_p = \frac{(Q_2 - Q_1)/Q_1}{(P_2 - P_1)/P_1}$$

The price elasticity of demand is usually negative because price increases tend to result in decreases in quantity demanded. This inverse relationship between price and quantity demanded, referred to as the **law of demand**, is representative of most products and services. However, the demand for products and services can demonstrate varying degrees of elasticity. The demand for products is said to be **elastic** if a percentage change in price results in a greater percentage change in quantity demanded. Conversely, the demand for products is said to be **inelastic** if a percentage change in price results in a smaller percentage change in quantity demanded. **Unitary elasticity** occurs when a percentage change in price results in an equal percentage change in quantity demanded. Figure 14-3 illustrates the relationships between price and quantity demanded under the three types of market structure.

Price Elasticity of Demand
In a market with elastic demand, consumers are price sensitive and any changes in price will cause total revenue to change in the opposite direction. Therefore, firms will tend to focus on ways to decrease price in an attempt to increase the quantity demanded and total revenue. In a market with inelastic demand, consumers are not sensitive to price changes and total revenue will change in the same direction. In this situation, firms will tend to focus on raising prices and total revenues, even with a decrease in quantity demanded. In markets with unitary demand, price changes have no effect on total revenue and firms should base pricing decisions on other factors such as cost.

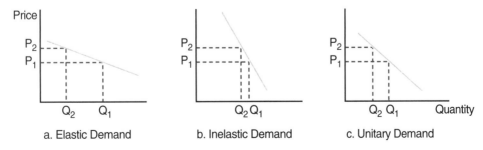

Figure 14-3 Price and Quantity Demand Comparison

Competitive Pricing

As the name implies, competitive pricing places the emphasis on price in relation to direct competition. Some firms allow others to establish prices and then position themselves accordingly (such as at, below, or above the competition). This method assures that the price charged for products and services will be within the same range as prices for competitive products in the immediate geographic area. This method does, however, have several drawbacks. First, consider the case of two similar firms, one is new and the other has been operating for several years. The new establishment is likely to have high fixed costs such as a mortgage with a high interest rate that must be paid each month. In contrast, the established firm might have a much lower mortgage payment each month and fewer costs than a firm starting a new business. Because of these differences, the established firm would have lower fixed operating expenses and could charge lower prices, even if all other expenses were equal. Second, other expenses might also vary among firms. Labor costs might be higher or lower depending on the skill level of the personnel, their length of service in the operation, and numerous other factors that may come into play. For this reason, it is extremely risky for managers to rely on the prices of a direct competitor when setting their own prices. Each operation is unique and has its own unique cost and profit structure. While management does need to monitor the competition, prices should never be based solely on prices charged by a competitor.

Price Segmentation

The importance of price varies among consumers, and firms often use this variation as a means for segmenting markets. Consequently, a firm can choose to target one or more of these markets with specific marketing strategies tailored to each market. The appropriate strategy will depend on the firm's costs, consumers' price sensitivities, and the competition. There are several tactics that can be used for segmenting markets on the basis of price.

Segmenting by Buyer Identification

One of the methods that can be used to segment by price is to base price on some form of buyer identification. That is, in order to obtain a discounted price, a buyer must belong to a certain group that shares similar characteristics. For example, hotels normally offer contract rates at a discount to corporations and government agencies. Government travelers are constrained by the per diem rates that are fixed by the government and many hotels price according to these rates, often at a significant discount relative to other groups. Similarly, contract food service providers may offer lower prices for nonprofit accounts (such as public schools) than for corporate accounts.

Segmenting by Purchase Location

It is possible to segment consumers based on where they purchase a product or service. Some restaurant chains will vary their prices in different geographic locations to account for differences in purchasing power and standard of living. For example, contract food service firms may charge more for accounts in large cities than for those in smaller cities. Similarly, prices may change by geographic location—accounts in the southern or midwestern United States have lower prices than accounts in the Northeast. Some of this is due to the demand, but there may be cost differences in the form of real estate and labor as well. Finally, most hotel, food service, and car rental firms charge different prices in international markets based on a country's standard of living.

Segmenting by Time of Purchase

Service firms tend to notice certain purchasing patterns based on the time of day, week, month, or year. Unfortunately, it is not always possible to meet the demand during these peak periods. One way to smooth the demand is to offer discounted prices at off-peak times. For example, large conference hotels are often willing to take SMERF groups, or other price sensitive associations, at significantly lower prices during off-peak seasons. This results in a shift in demand from peak times to off-peak times by the most price sensitive consumers.

Segmenting by Purchase Quantity

One of the most common forms of price segmentation is to vary price based on the quantity purchased, offering discounts for larger orders. The majority of firms, both small and large, will negotiate price discounts for larger volume orders. In particular, hotel salespeople are responsible for filling the hotel with groups by offering discounts that tend to increase with the size of the group. These discounts can be in the form of lower prices or concessions such as complimentary meeting space. Hotels and restaurants also use the same tactics to sell catering functions such as weddings and banquets.

Segmenting by Product Design

Another form of price segmentation is based on the actual product or service. It may be possible to segment consumers by offering simple variations of a firm's product or service that appeal to the different segments. For example, one hotel in Boston has different room categories based on the size and location of the room. There are traditional, deluxe, and executive rooms that can be offered to meeting planners at different rates. This allows the hotel to market to meeting segments with varying levels of price sensitivity such as corporate, government, and association. None of these variations have a significant impact on the cost of providing the service, but the hotel is able to charge significantly higher prices to a small segment of the market that values the additional amenities and services.

Segmenting by Product Bundling

The last form of price segmentation involves "packaging" products and services into price bundles. Offering several products at a packaged price can provide consumers with a better deal than if they were to purchase the bundle components separately. For example, tour operators combine the components of a vacation or trip (airfare, hotel, and tourist attractions) into a "package" that is sold to groups or individuals either directly, or through travel agents. An alternative form of product bundling is to offer premiums, or free merchandise, with the purchase. For example, many hotel chains offer meeting planners bonus points toward frequent guest or frequent flier programs if they book a meeting with one of the hotels in the chain.

These are some of the basic tactics that can be used to segment markets on the basis of price. The various tactics can be used alone, or in combination with one another, to achieve a firm's desired goals. Today's consumers can easily obtain information about competitive products and services, resulting in a large, value-conscious market. Firms will need to find ways to segment the price sensitive consumers from the quality-oriented consumers so that they can extract the most consumer surplus, and revenue, from the marketplace.

Price Negotiation

It is helpful to understand the role of price for each market segment when negotiating. Not all customers place the same importance on price, or have the same level of price sensitivity. Richard Harmer developed a Price-Segmentation Model that divided customers into four main price segments.[3] The segments are based on the relationship between the consumers' perceived pain of expenditure and perceived value of differentiation. The perceived pain of expenditure refers to both monetary and nonmonetary costs associated with making a purchase. The monetary cost is self-explanatory, and the nonmonetary costs consist of factors such as convenience and time, which also affect the pain of expenditure. The perceived value of differentiation refers to the extent to which consumers feel there are differences between the various brands or products competing in the marketplace. The four price segments appear in the table in Figure 14-4.

		Perceived Pain of Differentiation	
		Low	High
Perceived Pain of Expenditure	**High**	Price segment	Value segment
	Low	Convenience segment	Loyal segment

Figure 14-4 Price Segmentation Model

The **price segment** consists of buyers who choose to purchase products that have the lowest price consistent with some minimum level of acceptable quality. This segment is composed of large companies, government agencies, and price-conscious consumers. The larger entities normally qualify buyers based on minimum specifications and then proceed with a competitive bidding process. For example, contract food service firms normally bid for large institutional accounts, such as campus dining and employee cafeterias. The buyer is normally not willing to pay for incremental value. The following tactics may be useful in negotiating with this market segment.

- Refocus attention on product value and attempt to raise buyer's willingness to pay by justifying higher cost with added value.
- Participate selectively when the account will provide some incremental contribution and it does not undermine more profitable business.
- Use the "loss close" described in Chapter 9. Offer a low price (not in writing) and give a limited time frame for a response, after which the price is no longer valid.

It is important to remember that a firm can always return to this market segment, even if it chooses not to do business with them in the present. There is no loyalty and price is the main criterion.

The **value segment** consists of buyers who have limited resources and may be somewhat price sensitive, especially when making large expenditures. These buyers perceive some differences between brands and will shop for the best value (the price-quality trade-off). This is the fastest growing segment in the marketplace and it offers good profit potential for firms that can differentiate their products from the competition. The following strategies can be used.

- Negotiate with each buyer individually and try to maximize the value of your differentiation; extract the most consumer surplus possible.
- Salespeople need to distinguish between buyers who require a lower price to increase value, and those that require more quality through differentiation to increase value.
- Make sure that both parties understand which items are negotiable.

It is important to remember that this segment is much like the price segment because buyers have no predetermined loyalty or alliance with brands. They are looking for good deals (values) and tend to be somewhat price sensitive.

The **loyal segment** consists of buyers who have a strong preference for a particular brand because of its uniqueness and/or past experiences with the brand. This segment is not price sensitive as long as the price is below the buyer's reservation price (the maximum price the buyer is willing to pay). The loyal buyers tend to be risk averse and like to reduce the uncertainty surrounding the decision. The following negotiation tactics can prove useful with this segment.

- Maintain strong relationships by focusing on past performance.
- Stress the downside of purchasing an inferior product or service.
- Make it difficult to compare price and quality between suppliers; use price bundling.

This segment tends to thrive during the growth stage in the product life cycle, but it tends to gravitate toward the value segment as the market matures. In mature markets, there are more sellers with similar products and it is more difficult to differentiate.

The **convenience segment** consists of buyers who are not concerned with prices (as long as they are below the reservation price) and do not place great value on differentiation as long as the brand meets their minimum standards. There are not many tactics for negotiating with this segment because availability outweighs both price and value. For example, they feel that all hotels have beds and showers, food is food, and all airlines use the same planes. The seller's goal is to demonstrate that his or her product is the most convenient based on location and effort.

Finally, there are a few tactics that can be used for segments that show some price sensitivity. First, the "subtraction technique" involves decreasing the levels of some attributes to lower the cost of providing the product. This results in a lower priced version that can be justified because the buyer is sacrificing something in return. For example, hospitality and travel firms could require buyers to travel during non-peak periods to secure lower prices. Second, the "division technique" involves breaking down the overall cost of the item to a cost per unit. For example, a meeting planner could be shown that the cost of renting a meeting room is minimal per person and could easily be recouped in the registration fee.

Key Concepts

Chapter 14 discusses the concept of revenue management and the use of price negotiation in personal selling.

Revenue management is a form of selective discounting and is a valuable sales tool in services for several reasons:

- perishable inventory
- fluctuating demand
- ability to segment customers
- low variable costs

The goal of revenue management is to maximize a firm's actual revenue in relation to its potential revenue. Revenue per available room (REVPAR) and average daily rate (ADR) are used to measure a hotel's performance in regard to pricing. The following three approaches can be used by firms to set prices:

- cost-oriented pricing
- demand-oriented pricing
- competitive pricing

The importance of price varies among consumers, and firms often use this variation as a means for segmenting markets. There are several tactics that can be used for segmenting markets on the basis of price.

- segmenting by buyer identification
- segmenting by purchase location
- segmenting by time of purchase
- segmenting by purchase quantity
- segmenting by product design
- segmenting by product bundling

Finally, it is helpful to understand the role of price for each market segment when negotiating. Customers can be divided into four segments based on their perceived pain of expenditure and perceived value of differentiation.

- price segment
- value segment
- convenience segment
- loyal segment

Endnotes

[1] Smith, Barry C., John F. Leimkuler, and Ross M. Darrow (1992), "Yield Management at American Airlines," *Interfaces* 22 (1), 8-31.

[2] To further investigate these factors, see Cross, Robert G. (1997a), *Revenue Management*. New York: Broadway Books; Cross, Robert G. (1997b), "Launching the Revenue Rocket: How Revenue Management Can Work for Your Business," *Cornell Hotel and Restaurant Administration Quarterly* 38 (April), 32-43; Kimes, Sheryl E. (1989a), "Yield Management: A Tool for Capacity-Constrained Service Firms," *Journal of Operations Management* 8 (4), 348-363.

[3] Nagle, Thomas T. and Reed K. Holden (1995), *The Strategy and Tactics of Pricing*, 2nd edition, Englewood Cliffs, NJ: Prentice Hall, 163.

ANSWERS TO SELECTED EXERCISES

Chapter 3
Social Styles Exercise 1—Raymark Conference Center

a. Ms. Smith is timely, conservatively dressed, and not over friendly. Her office is "decorated" with number-oriented material and an Excel spreadsheet is visible on her computer screen. She studies the letters of testimony. The factors would indicate that Ms. Smith is likely an analytical style.

b. Your presentation should focus on facts, not small talk; maintain a sense of formality in your presentation. You should provide Ms. Smith with substantial amounts of data in writing, including advantages and disadvantages of your proposal, that she can examine. You must allow her adequate time for decision-making. Consequently, you should outline the steps of your proposal and detail the action plan, including dates. When the appointed date arrives, follow up with her and use a direct close.

c. This response will vary depending on your own social style.

Social Styles Exercise 2—USA Airlines

a. Mr. Larsen is somewhat late, and is casually dressed. His office has stacks of papers all around it, likely indicating numerous projects underway. He is very action-oriented as indicated by the photos in his office and his comment to the party on the phone. Finally, Mr. Larsen interrupts and asks a bottom-line question. All of these factors point to the fact that Mr. Larsen is likely a driver style.

b. Your presentation should provide the bottom-line first, then you should work backwards through your proposal to illustrate how the bottom-line was derived. You should focus on facts, but not be overly detailed; avoid chit-chat. Work to demonstrate that you are organized and that you value Mr. Larsen's time. Because Mr. Larsen is a driver, you should be prepared to gain commitment on the first call. Use a direct close.

c. This response will vary depending on your own social style.

Chapter 5
Identifying SPIN Questions Exercise

		SPIN Question Category
Seller:	As I understand it, you are doing all of your preventive maintenance projects on the plant equipment during the summer months, so that you are prepared for going on-stream by the fall season. Is that correct?	*Situation*
Seller:	How often do you have plant get-togethers, like picnics, parties, and banquets?	*Situation*
Seller:	How many people usually attend these events?	*Situation*
Seller:	Who usually organizes and caters your banquet?	*Situation*
Seller:	Are you happy with the arrangement?	*Problem*
Seller:	Do your guests that are staying in the hotel ever have trouble finding the location of the restaurant in town? For example, do some of the executives get lost and arrive late to the banquet?	*Problem*
Seller:	Does this lead to anxiety for your staff?	*Implication*
Seller:	If I can show you a way to reduce that stress would you be interested?	*Need-payoff*
Seller:	I'm sure your staff is outstanding in the way it executes day-to-day operations here at the plant, but, you indicated that you thought your staff was lacking in creativity for your Annual Safety Banquet. Is that right?	*Problem*
Seller:	As a result, Do you think that you are able to produce the full benefits of your banquets when they lack the creativity you are seeking?	*Problem*
Seller:	Well, does the theme for your banquet arouse excitement and motivation? Do your employees get pumped up about attending the banquet? Do they act in a more positive manner after the get-together?	*Implication*
Seller:	So, if I understand correctly, you are saying is that the Annual Safety Banquet may not generate all of the long-term effects you've been seeking. Is that right?	*Implication*
Seller:	If I can show you a way to maximize the utility from your get-togethers and to facilitate an increase in employee productivity afterward, would you be interested?	*Need-payoff*

Chapter 7
Owner Benefits/Product Characteristics Exercise

1. Owner benefit: ensure rave reviews
   Product characteristic: 'Hall of Mirrors' Ballroom

2. Owner benefit: increase traffic at your booth
   Product characteristic: provide complimentary coffee

3. Owner benefit: eliminate participant confusion and increase session participation
   Product characteristic: televising the session agenda

4. Owner benefit: reduce your company's business travel expenses
   Product characteristic: complimentary breakfast

5. Owner benefit: won't be embarrassed
   Product characteristic: automatic refill service

6. Owner benefit: reduce out-of-stocks and speed buffet service
   Product characteristic: increasing the entrée table

7. Owner benefit: company will save money and employees will be more comfortable
   Product characteristic: furnished corporate apartments

Chapter 14
Revenue Management Exercise

	Monday	Tuesday	Wednesday	Thursday
Occupancy rate	80%	100%	95%	85%
Group pattern (rooms)	50	100	100	100
Available rooms	100	0	25	75
Displaced rooms	0	100	75	25
Revenue from group	$5,000	$10,000	$10,000	$10,000
Displaced revenue	$0	$15,000	$11,250	$3,750
Net gain (loss)	$5,000	($5,000)	($1,250)	$6,250

Displacement effect = 5,000 − 5,000 − 1,250 + 6,250 = $5,000

Some of the other factors that should be considered are:

- the group room allotment set by the hotel
- additional revenues generated by the group or individuals (e.g., F&B, meeting room rental, etc.)
- potential for future revenues from the group or individuals
- current annual revenue generated by the group or individuals

REFERENCES

Boorom, Michael L., Jerry R. Goolsby, and Rosemary P. Ramsey. 1998. "Relational Communication Traits and their Effect on Adaptiveness and Sales Performance." *Journal of the Academy of Marketing Science* 26 (Winter): 16-30.

Brooks, Bill. 2000. "Listening Versus Talking: The Revolving Ratio." *The American Salesman* 45 (July): 20-23.

Calantone, Roger J., S. Tamer Cavusgil, and Yushan Zhao. 2002. "Learning Orientation, Firm Innovation Capability, and Firm Performance." *Industrial Marketing Management* 31 (September): 515-524.

Castleberry, Stephen B., C. David Shepherd, and Rick Ridnour. 1999. "Effective Interpersonal Listening in the Personal Selling Environment: Conceptualization, Measurement, and Nomological Validity." *Journal of Marketing Theory and Practice* 7 (Winter): 30-38.

Celuch, Kevin G., Chickery J. Kasouf, and Venkatakrisnan Peeruvemba. 2002. "The Effects of Perceived Market and Learning Orientation on Assessed Organizational Capabilities." *Industrial Marketing Management* 31 (September): 545-554.

Colquitt, Jason A. and Marcia J. Simmering. 1998. "Conscientiousness, Goal Orientation, and Motivation to Learn During the Learning Process: A Longitudinal Study." *Journal of Applied Psychology* 83 (August): 654-665.

Cronin, Ralph M. 1997. "The Telephone—Salesperson's Friend or Foe?" *The American Salesman* 42 (November): 23-28.

Cross, Robert G. 1997. *Revenue Management*. New York: Broadway Books.

Cross, Robert G. 1997. "Launching the Revenue Rocket: How Revenue Management Can Work for Your Business." *Cornell Hotel and Restaurant Administration Quarterly* 38 (April): 32-43.

Deshpande, Rohit, John U. Farley, and Frederick E. Webster. 1993. "Corporate Culture, Customer Orientation, and Innovativeness in Japanese Firms: A Quadrad Analysis," *Journal of Marketing* 57 (January): 23-27.

Feiertag, Howard. 1992. "Mishandled Inquiries Are Lost Opportunities." *Hotel and Motel Management* 207 (August 16): 13.

Feiertag, Howard. 1993. "Rig Up More Business by Improving Phone Procedures." *Hotel and Motel Management* 208 (August 16): 13.

Feiertag, Howard. 1998. "How Much Business Did You Lose Today?" *Hotel and Motel Management* 213 (March 2): 58.

Futrell, Charles M. 1996. *Fundamentals of Selling: Customers for Life*. Chicago, IL: The McGraw-Hill Companies, Inc.: 243.

Futrell, Charles. 1997. *ABC's of Relationship Selling*. 5th ed. Chicago: Irwin.

Goolsby, Jerry R., Rosemary R. Lagace, and Michael L. Boorom. 1992. "Psychological Adaptiveness and Sales Performance." *Journal of Personal Selling & Sales Management* 12 (Spring): 51-66.

Graham, John R. 1995. "The 12 Deadly Sins." *Manager's Magazine* 70 (December): 12.

Grewal, Dhruv and Arun Sharma. 1991. "The Effect of Salesforce Behavior on Customer Satisfaction: An Interactive Framework." *Journal of Personal Selling & Sales Management* 11 (Summer): 13-23.

Gschwandtner, Gerhad. 1982. "Closing Sales via Body Signals." *Marketing Times* 29 (September/October): 12-13.

Hawes, John M., Kenneth E. Mast, and John E. Swan. 1989. "Trust Earning Perceptions of Sellers and Buyers." *The Journal of Personal Selling & Sales Management* 9 (Spring): 1-8.

Heiman, Stephen E., Diane Sanchez, with Tad Tuleja. 1998. *The New Strategic Selling*. New York: Warner Books.

Hopkins, Tom. 1995. *Selling for Dummies*. Foster City, CA: IDG Books Worldwide.

Ismail, Ahmed. 1999. *Hotel Sales & Operations*. Albany: Delmar Publishers.

Johnston, Wesley J. and Jeffrey E. Lewin. 1996. "Organizational Buying Behavior: Toward an Integrative Framework." *Journal of Business Research* 35 (January): 1-15.

Kimes, Sheryl E. 1989. "Yield Management: A Tool for Capacity-Constrained Service Firms." *Journal of Operations Management* 9 (4): 348-363.

Kotler, Philip, John Bowen, and James Makens. 2003. *Marketing for Hospitality and Tourism*. 3rd ed. Upper Saddle River, NJ: Prentice Hall.

Leone, Patrick. 2002. "The Right Way to Get Referrals." *Advisor Today* (October): 84.

Lichtenthal, J. David. 1988. "Group Decision Making in Organizational Buying: A Role Structure Approach." *Advances in Business Marketing*. vol. 3. ed. Arch G. Woodside. Greenwich, CT: JAI Press: 119-157.

Lilien, Gary L. and M. Anthony Wong. 1984. "Exploratory Investigation of the Structure of the Buying Center in the Metalworking Industry." *Journal of Marketing Research* 21 (February): 1-11.

Lorge, Sarah. 1998. "Selling101: The Best Way to Prospect." *Sales and Marketing Management*, (January): 80.

Marchetti, Michele. 1996. "Talking Body Language." *Sales and Marketing* 148 (October): 46.

McGarvey, Robert. 1996. "Listen Up!" *Entrepreneur* August: 104-110.

McQuiston, Daniel H. and Peter R. Dickson. 1991. "The Effect of Perceived Personal Consequences on Participation and Influence in Organizational Buying." *Journal of Business Research* 23 (September): 159-177.

Merrill, David and Roger Reid. 1981. *Personal Styles and Effective Performance: Make Your Style Work for You*. Radnor, PA: Chilton.

Metcalf, Tom. 1997. "Communication Your Message: The Hidden Dimension." *Life Association News* 92 (April): 18-21.

Metcalf, Tom. 1997. "Listening to Your Clients." *Life Association News* 92 (July): 16-17.

Morgan, Jim. 1997. "The Best Sales Reps Follow Up on their Suggestions." *Purchasing* 123 (November 27): 65-68.

Nagle, Thomas T. and Reed Holden. 1995. *The Strategy and Tactics of Pricing*. 2nd edition. Englewood Cliffs, NJ: Prentice Hall: 163.

Piscitelli, Paul. 1997. "How to Wow an Audience." *Sales and Marketing Management*. 149 (June): 63-68.

Rackham, Neil. 1998. *Spin Selling*. New York: McGraw-Hill.

Saxe, Robert and Barton A. Weitz. 1982. "The SOCO Scale: A Measure of the Customer Orientation of Salespeople." *Journal of Marketing Research* 19 (August): 343-351.

Sheth, Jagdish N. 1966. "Organizational Buying Behavior: Past Performance and Future Expectations." *Journal of Business and Industrial Marketing* 11 (3-4): 7-24.

Sheth, Jagdish N. 1973. "A Model of Industrial Buyer Behavior." *Journal of Marketing* 37 (October): 50–56.

Smith, Barry C., John F. Leimkuler, and Ross M. Darrow. 1992. "Yield Management at American Airlines." *Interfaces* 22 (1): 8-31.

Spiro, Rosann L. and Barton A. Weitz. 1990. "Adaptive Selling: Conceptualization, Measurement and Nomological Validity." *Journal of Marketing Research* 27 (February): 61-69.

Successful Meetings. 2003. "Meeting Market Outlook: Size of the Market." VNU eMedia Inc. [online at <http://www.successmtgs.com/successmtgs/images/pdf/sm_market overview.pdf>].

Webster, Frederick E., Jr. and Yoram Wing. 1972. *Organizational Buying Behavior*. Englewood Cliffs, NJ: Prentice-Hall.

Weitz, Barton A., Sujan and Sujan. 1986. "Knowledge, Motivation, and Adaptive Behavior: A Framework for Improving Selling Effectiveness." *Journal of Marketing* 50 (October): 174-191.

Williams, Michael R. and Jill S. Attaway. 1996. "Exploring Salespersons' Customer Orientation as a Mediator of Organization Culture's Influence on Buyer-Seller Relationships." *Journal of Personal Selling & Sales Management* 16 (Fall): 33-52.

Woodside Arch G. 1992. "Conclusions on Mapping How Industry Buys," *Advances in Business Marketing and Purchasing*. vol. 5. ed. Arch G. Woodside. Greenwich, CT: JAI Press: 283-300.

INDEX